i ❤ patchwork

21 IRRESISTIBLE ZAKKA PROJECTS TO SEW

RASHIDA COLEMAN-HALE

INTERWEAVE.
interweavestore.com

Editor: Katrina Loving
Art Director: Karla Baker
Photography: Joe Hancock
Illustrations: Ann Swanson
Stylist: Pam Chavez
Production: Katherine Jackson

Interweave Press LLC
201 East Fourth Street
Loveland, CO 80537
interweavestore.com

Printed in China by Asia Pacific Offset. Ltd.

Library of Congress
Cataloging-in-Publication Data
Coleman-Hale, Rashida.
 I love patchwork! : 21 irresistible Zakka
projects to sew / Rashida Coleman-Hale.
 p. cm.
 Includes index.
 ISBN 978-1-59668-142-2 (pbk.)
 1. Patchwork. 2. Sewing--Japan. 3. Deco-
ration and ornament--Japan. I. Title.
 TT835.C6472 2009
 746.46--dc22

 2009009433

 10 9 8 7 6 5 4 3 2 1

ACKNOWLEDGMENTS

Wow, has this ever been a journey!

Huge, huge, tremendous thanks to:

- Editorial director Tricia Waddell, for giving me the opportunity to share my knowledge and for believing in my work. Thank you so much! You're truly a kindred spirit.

- My editor Katrina Loving for all of your hard work and being oh so patient during my space-cadet moments. Thank you, thank you, thank you.

- Charlene, for all of the late night chats and support all the way from Singapore. *Feichang xiexie!*

- Lea, you're like a sister. Thank you for all of your wisdom.

- Mommie, for dragging me to the sewing machine so many years ago.

- Grandma and Grandpa, for just being you and being there for me.

- My sweet husband, Mel. You've been my rock through all of this, thank you for being so supportive and coming along for this wild ride.

- Dad, Verna, Rosalinda, Fernando, Donna, Brice, Gretta, Brandi, Ton, Chris, Darlene, and Darielle for being so supportive and believing in me.

- And finally all of my bloggy buddies, there are too many to name! Thank you for all of your encouraging e-mails and comments—they really kept me going!

dedication

To my sweet Isabella and Elijah
Life is filled with possibilities.
With all my love, Mommy

introduction

One summer, many years ago, my mother decided that she was going to continue a long family tradition and teach me how to sew. She and her sister had learned to sew many years before from their father, a tailor, and their mother and grandmother, who sewed as well. The first thing that popped into my head was "Why would I want to do that?" My mother basically had to drag me over to the sewing machine. I was miserable, and I'm pretty sure I pouted and rolled my eyes every step of the way, not realizing that sewing would eventually change my life. Through sewing, I discovered a new world, which eventually led me to attend the Fashion Institute of Technology, where I studied fashion design. Now, I can't live without sewing, and I do it every chance I get.

I fell in love with patchwork some time later, when I was expecting my daughter. The colors, oh the colors—how they thrilled me! I couldn't wait to learn more and explore all of the possibilities. I was lucky enough to spend some time in Japan, where I learned to appreciate the beauty of handmade *Zakka*. For those of you new to the Japanese term, most Japanese/English dictionaries have translated the word to mean "miscellaneous goods." That vague definition of the term has expanded and evolved over the years and Zakka is now understood as an aesthetic and design style, mainly focused on household items that enhance one's environment. I like to refer to all of the wonderful things that we have in our homes to spruce up our daily lives as Zakka. Be it handmade or store-bought, it can be anything from a set of coasters to a tissue box holder, wooden spoons, cute little figurines, even something as simple as an empty jam jar. A lot of handmade Zakka is created with linen and has an organic look. I've learned to make some fun projects by marrying the Zakka world with my love of patchwork.

Patchwork doesn't have to be complicated to achieve innovative, modern, and amazing results. I will show you how to make fun, simple projects by combining linen and cotton print fabrics using some simple techniques. I hope the projects in this book will inspire you to explore all of the possibilities in the patchwork Zakka world. You can keep a project simple and plain or embellish to your heart's desire and create your own personalized style. Soon you will be creating patchwork Zakka for yourself and your loved ones.

tools and materials

Every sewist has to have what seems like an arsenal of tools and materials at their disposal for successful creating. This is an overview of the essential tools and materials for creating the projects in this book, as well as a few nonessential, but very helpful tools.

You should always have the following items on hand before beginning any of the projects in this book. Anything further that is needed will be listed with each project.

Sewing machine (with assorted needles and presser feet, see Sewing Machine below)

Handsewing needles

Assorted sewing thread (to match or coordinate with your fabric[s])

Straight pins

Pincushion

Fabric scissors

Craft scissors

Embroidery scissors or other small, sharp scissors

Rotary cutter and self-healing mat

Seam ripper

Clear gridded acrylic ruler

Tape measure

Iron and ironing board

Water-soluble fabric pen and/or tailor's chalk

Pencil

Sewing Machine

There are so many different types of sewing machines on the market, some are very simple, while others look as if they could be time machines, sporting tons of special features. It can make shopping for a new machine seem quite daunting, but it doesn't have to be. Although some of those bells and whistles can be a lot of fun, a good basic machine is really all you need.

For the projects in this book, your machine should have the following:

- Adjustable stitch length and width
- Backtack (p. 154) function
- Zigzag stitch (p. 155) setting and zigzag foot (not shown): This is usually the standard presser foot.
- Zipper foot (not shown)
- Buttonhole function and buttonhole foot (not shown)

- Walking foot: This foot grips multiple layers of fabric, which is helpful for quilting and it can also be used for sewing binding.
- Blind hem foot or edgestitch foot: Both of these have a metal guide that can be placed along an edge or a fold, making edgestitching easier (a blind hem foot comes with some machines).

I have a Janome that I purchased online from one of those sew and vacuum type of stores. I love it immensely, and I treat it like it's one of my children. It has all the features I want and runs like a dream. When

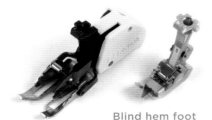

Blind hem foot

Walking foot

tip Because every machine is a little different, be sure to always have your sewing machine manual on hand for information about settings and using the different functions on your machine.

purchasing your own sewing machine be sure to shop around. Go to a store or a dealer and sit down with some machines, inspect the features, and ask questions. Just make sure that your sewing machine will fit your needs.

Once you have your machine home, be sure to clean it often, freeing it from dust and lint that can accumulate from regular use. Your machine should come equipped with tools for cleaning, and the manual will instruct you on how to keep it in tip-top shape. Finally, take your machine in to the dealer or shop for a tune-up once a year. These simple tasks can help your machine live a longer, happier sewing life.

Sewing Machine Needles

These needles come in a variety of sizes, each for a specific task; refer to your sewing-machine manual for information on the needles that came with your machine and/or specialized needles. Universal point needles are the all-purpose needle, good for just about any type of sewing.

It's important that you change your needle often. I've found that a good rule of thumb is to change your needle before each project.

Have additional sets on hand since needles do indeed get dull and sometimes even break. Most machines come with an extra set of needles along with the one that's already attached, but you can buy additional sets as well. Check your sewing-machine manual to be sure you're buying the right type for your machine.

Bobbins

I always have several of these wound up and ready to go next to my machine. Having to stop in the middle of sewing to wind a new bobbin is really no fun. So buy a few extra empty ones to keep on hand. Be sure to check your sewing-machine manual so that you buy the right size for your machine.

Straight Pins

Straight seams make for happy patchwork, and pinning is the key to straight seams. There are several types of straight pins available, but glass-head pins are my favorite, hands down. You can press over them with a hot iron and they flow through fabric with brilliant ease. Glass-heads may cost a little more, but they're well worth it to me. They are available in a variety of colors, but I'd avoid buying the clear ones, as they are difficult to find if you lose one.

Handsewing Needles

There are so many types of handsewing needles, all with a different use. Sharps are a great general-purpose needle to have in your sewing arsenal. They can be used for general sewing, appliqué, and even quilting. Although a thimble isn't essential, it's a nice thing to have around for handsewing. If you need to push the needle through several layers of fabric, your finger will thank you for using a thimble.

Pincushion

Having a pincushion is an absolute necessity for holding your pins and needles. There are many different types of pincushions available for purchase in a plethora of sizes, shapes, and colors. You can also make your own quite easily. I've always been annoyed by my pincushions sliding around when I'm trying to pin them. My Blossom Pincushion project solved that problem (see p. 71)!

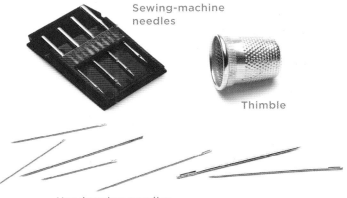

Sewing-machine needles

Thimble

Handsewing needles

Seam rippers

Embroidery scissors

Fabric shears

Thread nippers

Hera marker

Point turner/seam creaser

Thread

Since I typically only use cotton or linen fabric for my projects, I stick to cotton thread for general sewing and silk thread for appliqué. Although polyester thread is indeed strong, it can actually cut through the fibers in cotton fabric. The only brand of cotton thread that I use is Mettler Silk-Finish Cotton. I find it to be far superior to other brands, and I love how it looks on my projects.

Test out a few brands and see which ones tickle your fancy. Try your best to avoid cheap thread as it tends to break easily and can get a little fuzzy during use.

Seam Ripper

Having to undo a seam is something we all wish we could avoid, but mistakes do happen. You'll need a sharp seam ripper to cut through the threads of the faulty seam. I prefer the larger more heavy-duty seam rippers because I'm the girl who always ends up breaking the small plastic ones. You don't want to be that girl.

Scissors

Most crafters have several pairs of scissors and use each for a different purpose. I have three pairs that I use most frequently:

- Knife-edge bent shears for cutting fabric.
- Embroidery scissors for cutting thread and clipping fabric in tight spots.
- Craft Scissors (not shown) for cutting paper and everything else.

Find scissors that are comfortable and feel good in your hand. You may want to splurge a little when buying scissors because you'll be using them quite a bit. Better-quality scissors will also last longer, and they won't dull as quickly as the lower-quality ones. Scissors will dull over time, so you will need to be sure to have them sharpened now and then.

Thread Nippers

Although not essential, thread nippers are handy for clipping threads when you've finished a seam. If you're as graceful as I am, you'll probably like to have a pair of these to avoid regrettable mistakes that can happen when trying to use regular scissors for such close snipping.

Rotary Cutter and Self-Healing Mat

Sometimes I think I use my rotary cutter even more than my scissors. This tool makes sewing life easier by allowing you to cut quickly through several layers of fabric at a time. There are a variety of rotary cutters available, in a variety of sizes. I have an Olfa 45mm, which is a good all-purpose size. I also have an Olfa

Self-healing mat

Rotary cutters

18mm, which is better for cutting smaller pieces and curves. These blades are super sharp, so make sure that the one you choose has some type of safety feature. Have a few replacement blades handy as well. The cutter blades can get dull with use. Pinking blades are also available from some brands, and I tend to use them more often than pinking shears.

Remember to protect your cutting blades and tabletops from damage with a self-healing mat. They come in several sizes and can sometimes be bought as a kit with the rotary cutter. An 18" x 24" (45.5 x 61 cm) mat is a good size for starting out, but you may soon find that you'd prefer a larger one for various projects.

Clear Gridded Acrylic Ruler

You'll need one or two of these to use with your rotary cutter to make straight cuts. It is an indispensable tool for creating beautiful patchwork. They come in various sizes and colors, but I find the Omnigrid 6" x 12" (15 x 30.5 cm) and 6" x 24" (15 x 61 cm) versions to be the most useful. Try a few out and see which ones suit you best.

Iron and Ironing Board

One of the first things I do when I'm preparing to sew is turn on my iron. Linen and cotton like to wrinkle, so I'm constantly ironing. You don't need to have an extra-fancy iron, but make sure that you can switch the steam on and off and that it has an adjustable temperature setting for ironing various fabrics. Having an automatic turn-off feature is a bonus, especially if you sometimes forget to turn things off. Be good to your iron because a leaky iron or one with burnt or sticky

buildup could easily ruin a precious project, and there is nothing more frustrating than that.

Tape Measure

These are great for quick measurements while you're sewing. You should have one that's at least 60" (152.5 cm) in length. I've used the type that you can drape around your neck, but for some reason I always end up cutting one of the ends off with my rotary cutter. I solved that problem by buying a Clover retractable tape measure, which also has metric scaling on the back. It's up to you which type you decide to use, just keep it away from your rotary blade!

Marking Tools

There has been much debate about which product is the best for marking lines on fabric. There really is no perfect solution and each way has its benefits and its drawbacks. I suggest always testing on a scrap of fabric before you start marking up your project and make sure you follow manufacturer's instructions to avoid mishaps (for example, some marks become permanent when ironed). Here are the tools I most frequently use:

- Water-soluble fabric pen (not shown) for temporary marks on fabric that can be "erased" with water (recommended: C over Chaco Pen).
- Tailor's chalk pencil (not shown) for temporary marks on fabric that can just be brushed away.
- Mechanical pencil (never needs sharpening; not shown) for tracing templates and making notes.
- Hera marker, a tool for making creases in fabric to mark lines or shapes.

Bone Folder (Seam Creaser) / Point Turner

A bone folder is a nifty little tool that is used for paper crafts to set creases and score card stock or cardboard. It can help to create crisp, professional looking folds. A point turner is a tool with a pointed end that is used to push out corners and smooth out seams for crisp, neat edges and corners. A bluntly pointed object, such as a knitting needle, can also be used for this purpose. Often, the same tool can be used for both purposes. They are sometimes sold as point turners/seam creasers.

the stash:
FABRICS and CARE

Ah, fabric. It's the real reason we all love to sew so much, isn't it? I have to admit that I really, really have to show some restraint when it comes to fabric shopping. Fabric Addicts Anonymous anyone?

Aside from your local quilting and fabric shop, there are a plethora of shops on the Internet from which one can purchase fabric. I've listed a few of my favorites for you in the Resources section on p. 158. There are also some great vintage finds to be had at your local thrift shop, garage and estate sales, craigslist.org, and even Ebay.

My favorite fabrics by far are 100% linen and 100% cotton; they are what I use for all of my projects. Feel free to experiment with different types of fabrics to achieve a look that's all your own as you create the projects in this book.

Linen

Linen, how do I love thee. Let me count the ways. Working with linen just makes me divinely and utterly happy. This fabric, much like cotton, is very easy to work with and can be used for just about any project. Natural linen comes in lovely subtle shades of beige and cream, which looks wonderful paired up with some colorful patchwork. Linen and cotton make a great team!

Made from the stalk of the flax plant, linen is two to three times stronger than cotton and is also extremely absorbent. Linen can absorb 30% or more of its weight in moisture, which makes it especially useful for making things like kitchen towels and summer clothing (it will pull moisture away from the skin during the hotter seasons).

Should you decide to buy your linen online, I suggest ordering swatches before you buy several yards. It's hard to see the quality of the linen in photos. Lower-quality linen tends to be a bit slubby, meaning there are lumps and bumps in the threads. Higher-quality linen is very smooth and consistent in texture and appearance throughout.

You can buy linen in the same types of cuts as quilting fabric (see 100% Cotton at right). It is also available in the following weights and is typically 60" (152.5 cm) wide.

Handkerchief-weight: 3 to 4 oz
Slightly sheer, this weight is suitable for handkerchiefs, sheer curtains, and light blouses.

Medium-weight: 4½ to 6½ oz
My favorite weight to work with, this weight can be used for almost any type of project from clothing to interior projects. Both medium- and heavyweight are excellent choices for embroidery. Medium-weight linen is appropriate for any of the projects in this book.

Heavyweight: 7 to 8 oz
Suitable for upholstery and curtains, I like to use this weight for tote bags as well.

Care

If the project you are making is going to be washed a lot, I highly recommend preshrinking your fabric in the wash before sewing, as linen will definitely suffer initial shrinkage.

For the maximum shrinkage, linen should be washed on a hot setting and then dried on a low setting or line dried. You may want to wash it a few times to make sure it won't shrink more. You'll be happy that you did.

You'll notice when purchasing linen that it has a very stiff and crisp hand when it's fresh off of the bolt. This can be great for certain projects, and if you'd like the fabric to maintain that feel, then washing isn't recommended, and dry cleaning would be the better choice. The more linen is hand- or machine-washed the softer and less stiff it becomes. I've found that linen also responds well to spray starch, and it will help in keeping the stiffer hand if that's what you prefer. When washing a finished project, wash it in cold water as opposed to using hot water as you did when preshrinking.

Linen wrinkles quite easily, and some people feel the wrinkles add to it's charm. But, I like my work to be wrinkle-free, so I iron it like mad. To iron the linen, dampen it with a spray bottle of water and iron it on a high steam setting. Don't worry about scorching it, linen has a very high resistance to heat, but it does tend to develop a shine when ironed too much. To remedy that, simply use a press cloth over the linen to protect it as you iron (muslin or scrap cotton fabric works well for this, cotton press cloths are also available for purchase at many fabric stores).

100% Cotton

Plain-weave quilter's cotton is, in my opinion, the easiest cotton to work with. It feels great to the touch, can be washed easily, is very easy to cut and sew, and is great for patchwork. It does like to wrinkle, so be sure to have your iron ready!

This cotton can be bought in 42″ (106.5), 44″ (112 cm), or 54″ (137 cm) widths, but you'll probably find that 44″ (112 cm) is the most common width.

In addition to fabric by the yard (and/or fractions of a yard), many shops also have fat cuts available. These are regular cuts of fabric, cut off of the bolt and then cut in half, parallel to the selvedge. There are two types of fat cuts: **fat quarters**, which are 18″ x 22″ (45.5 x 56 cm) and **fat eighths,** which are 9″ x 22″ (23 x 56 cm). Some fabric shops sell these in sweet little bundles, which are great for stash building.

If you're like me, you probably like to buy fabric whether you need it or not, but if shopping for a particular project, try to determine how much fabric you will need in advance. It's never a bad idea to buy a little more than what you need in case of mistakes and that darn shrinkage! The wonderful thing about the projects in this book is that many of them require various small pieces, so you'll probably be able to use up lots of scraps from your current stash.

Care

Cotton fabric likes to shrink! So it is essential to wash your fabric before you begin cutting it. This will allow you to avoid any disappointment that would likely be the result of waiting to wash a finished project, only to find that it's become warped. Cold water works best for cotton as hot water can be damaging to the color or finish.

Storage

Keeping your stash clean and dust free is important for the longevity of the fabric. Avoiding direct sunlight is important as well to avoid fading. The linen closet at my house has been turned into the "fabric-stashery." The sheets and towels will just have to fend for themselves. I like to keep my fabrics folded neatly and color coordinated on a shelf. Having my fabric folded and organized makes it much easier for me to see what I have when choosing fabric for a new project. The color coordination aspect is helpful as well. If I have color combinations in mind, I don't have to spend much time searching. This method may not work for you, just find a storage place that is clean and dry and organize according to your own preferences.

Choosing Colors and Prints

Selecting colors is one of the best parts of starting a new project—it's just so much fun! I simply choose one print fabric as my base, and I select the other colors based on those in the base fabric. The colors you choose don't have to exactly match the colors in your base fabric either. I've always been pleased with the results I get by choosing several fabrics in varying shades of the same or similar colors.

There is no written rule for choosing prints, at least not to my knowledge. With the growing number of fabric designers and different prints available, you can go to town mixing and matching all the prints you want. I'm especially fond of polka dots, stripes, and gingham prints. I find that they help the other prints really pop on a project, so I typically use them as accent fabrics or as a lining for my pouches and bags.

Don't be afraid to experiment with color combinations and prints, try something unexpected—you'll be pleasantly pleased by the results.

techniques

Before you begin the projects in this book there are a few basic techniques that you should learn for creating beautiful patchwork projects. Just remember, it takes some practice—take your time, there's no rush!

Squaring Up

One of the first things you need to do with your fabric is straighten the edges so that you can make nice straight cuts. Squaring up is essential for accurate patchwork piecing and will save you a lot of heartache later on. Grab your rotary cutter, self-healing mat, two clear acrylic rulers (the 6" x 12" [15 x 30.5 cm] and the 6" x 24" [15 x 61 cm]) and your fabric, then follow the instructions below for squaring up.

1 First, iron your fabric to ensure that it is nice and flat when you're ready to cut.

2 Fold the fabric in half, wrong sides together, matching up the selvedges; place it on the self-healing mat. (Sometimes the selvedges won't line up perfectly, and that's okay). The fold should be facing you, toward the bottom of the mat, with the selvedges facing toward the top.

3 Place the 6" x 24" (15 x 61 cm) ruler (or the larger of the two that you own) on top of the fabric at one side (the left or right cut edge), overlapping the edge of the fabric by 1" (2.5 cm). Line up one of the horizontal grid lines on the ruler with the fold of the fabric (**figure 1**).

4 Place the second ruler right next to the first, on top of the fabric. The edges of the rulers should be touching, and a horizontal line on each should be in line with the fold (**figure 2**). Adjust placement of fabric as necessary until the fold is in line with both of the grid lines.

5 Remove the second ruler and place your hand firmly on top of first ruler to keep it in place. Use the edge of the ruler as a guide to make a straight cut (mind your fingers!) by running your rotary cutter flush against the edge. Cut the fabric all the way from the folded edge to the selvedge (**figure 3**). Voila! You now have a perfectly squared edge. You'll want to start your cutting from this edge, cutting strips to the necessary width (see Cutting Shapes at right). Check to make sure that the cut edge of the fabric is at a perfect right angle to the fold before cutting each strip. If not, you'll need to square up again before cutting.

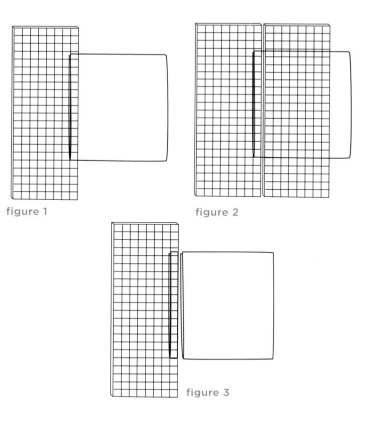

figure 1

figure 2

figure 3

Cutting Shapes

For some of the projects in this book, you'll need to cut squares, rectangles, and triangles. Several squares and rectangles can easily be cut with accuracy from strips of your squared-up fabric, while triangles can quickly be created from squares.

note

The following instructions for cutting shapes include adding seam allowance. The templates and cutting measurements for the projects in this book already have seam allowance added, so you don't need to worry about adding it when you are cutting your shapes. Simply use the templates and/or measurements as given.

Squares

1 Cut strips of squared-up (see p. 14) fabric to the width you'd like your finished squares to be plus ½" (1.3 cm) for seam allowance. For example, if your finished squares need to be 5" x 5" (12.5 x 12.5 cm), you'll cut your strips 5½" (14 cm) wide.

2 Now, use your ruler to measure the length of the squares (desired finished length plus ½" (1.3 cm) seam allowance) along the squared-up edges of the strip and cut (use the edge of your ruler as a guide to make straight cuts with the rotary cutter).

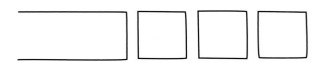

Rectangles

1 Cut strips of squared-up fabric to the width you'd like your finished rectangles to be plus ½" (1.3 cm) seam allowance. For example, if your finished rectangles need to be 5" (12.5 cm) long x 7" (18 cm) wide, you'll cut your strips 7½" (19 cm) wide.

2 Now use your ruler to measure the length of the rectangles (desired finished length plus ½" (1.3 cm) seam allowance) along the squared-up edges of the strip and cut (use the edge of your ruler as a guide to make straight cuts with the rotary cutter).

Half-Square Triangles

Measuring for these is a little different than for the Squares and Rectangles so be sure to read the instructions carefully!

1 Half-square triangles are simply made from squares that are cut diagonally in half. Cut strips of squared-up fabric to the width you'd like your finished triangles to be plus ⅞" (2.2 cm) for seam allowance. For example, if your finished triangles need to be 5" (12.55 cm) wide, you'll cut your strip 5⅞" (15 cm) wide.

2 Now, use your ruler to measure the length of the triangles (the same measurement as the width) along the squared up edges of the strip and cut (use the edge of your ruler as a guide to make straight cuts with the rotary cutter).

3 Place your ruler on one of the squares diagonally from corner to corner and cut it in half along the edge of the ruler. You'll have two beautifully made triangles of equal size. Repeat to cut the remaining squares into triangles.

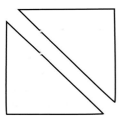

Pinning

Pinning is something that I really didn't enjoy doing until I began my love affair with patchwork. Now, I've come to realize that it's an absolute must for perfect patchwork seams. It's a simple task that sometimes gets overlooked, but pinning properly before you begin to sew will make all the difference. There may be times when you don't need to pin, but be sure to pin when matching seams to ensure accurate patchwork. Keep your pincushion nearby and remember to remove the pins as you sew. You can easily damage your sewing machine or break a needle by sewing over a pin.

Basic Pinning

Place your fabric right sides together, lining up the raw edges, then insert your pins through all layers, perpendicular to the raw edges.

A good rule of thumb is to place your pins about 2″ (5 cm) apart on straight edges, moving them a little closer together on curved edges. Be sure that the ball ends of the pins are pointing away from the fabric for easy removal as you sew.

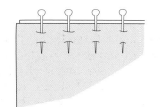

Patchwork Pinning

1 Before you begin stitching 2 units together, press the corresponding seam allowances on the seam(s) of each unit in opposite directions. This will ensure that the two edges will meet perfectly when you pin and stitch them together.

2 Place the 2 units right sides together and line up any corresponding seams (you can feel with your fingers if the seams are touching).

3 Pin the 2 units together, with the pins perpendicular to the raw edge and be sure to pin about $\frac{1}{8}$″ (3 mm) to each side of the matched seams to hold them firmly in place. Leave the ball ends of the pins out of the fabric a bit for easy removal as you sew.

Handsewing

Handsewing isn't very difficult to learn and can be enjoyable as well as relaxing. I learned how to handsew from my grandmother who sewed her own curtains, pillows, school uniforms for her children, and even mattresses—all by hand!

In this section, I'll cover some of the handsewing basics that you'll need to complete the projects in this book. See the Glossary on p. 156 for instructions on the handstitches used in this book.

Preparing Your Thread

With sharp scissors, cut one strand of thread, no longer than the length of your arm (or about 18" [45.5 cm]). Cutting it any longer than that will most likely cause your thread to get unpleasantly tangled. Using some Thread Heaven or beeswax to coat the thread can help make the thread less likely to tangle and will make threading a little easier. (Thread Heaven and beeswax can both be found packaged in small containers that are designed for coating the thread. Follow manufacturer's instructions to coat the thread.)

Pass the thread through the eye of the needle and pull several inches of thread through the eye, creating a tail. You should thread your needle with one strand of thread for most handstitches, but when the sewing requires stronger stitching you should use the thread doubled by knotting the ends together.

Knotting the Thread

My grandmother taught me one way to knot the end of my thread, and the quilter's knot is an alternative that I've picked up in the last couple of years. You can use either method, try them both and see which you prefer.

Grandma's knot

1 Hold the tail of your thread between your thumb and your forefinger and wrap the thread around your finger. Cross the thread over the end you're holding and slip it between your thumb and forefinger.

2 Begin rolling the thread up your finger with your thumb until it slips off of your finger, then slide the knot toward the end of the thread (it will tighten into a secure knot at the end of the thread).

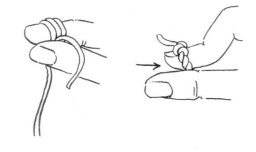

Quilter's knot

1 Thread the needle and then grasp the eye of the needle with the thumb and forefinger of your non-dominant hand. Bring the long end of the thread up so that the point of the needle and the end of the thread are facing each other and then slip the end of the thread between the fingers that are holding the eye of the needle (you now have a loop of thread hanging from the needle; **figure 1**).

2 With your free hand, wrap the tail of the longer thread around the needle three times (**figure 2**).

3 Slide the wound thread down and lodge it between the fingers holding the eye of the needle and then, with your free hand, slowly pull the needle from the pointed end (**figure 3**), until the entire length of thread has passed through your thumb and forefinger (still grasping the wound thread). The wound thread will form a small knot at the base of the thread.

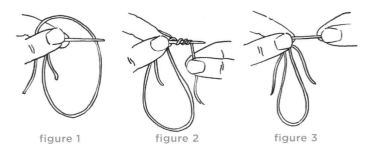

figure 1   figure 2   figure 3

Machine Sewing

Machine sewing can bring you so much joy, as it enables you to create projects quickly and with ease. Take some time to sit and read your sewing machine manual so that you can really get to know your machine and all of its many functions. The more familiar you are with your machine and how it operates, the easier it will be for you to sew with speed and accuracy.

Some Notes About Seam Allowance

Patchwork uses $1/4''$ (6 mm) seam allowances and ensuring that your seam allowances remain accurate will allow your pieces to be smooth and fit together nicely. There are a couple of ways you can be sure to have the perfect $1/4''$ (6 mm) seam allowances:

The Throat Plate

The throat plate of your sewing machine (the plate, usually metal, that lies directly beneath your presser foot and needle) typically has marks on it that you can use as a guide while sewing. If your machine does not have these marks, you can use a piece of masking tape to create a seam guide on the throat plate. This guide will help you sew a straight seam, exactly $1/4''$ (6 mm) from the raw edges.

Create a Seam Guide

1 Take a piece of $1/4''$ (6 mm) graph paper (four squares to an inch) and trim it along the edge of one of the graph lines at the right side of the paper to ensure an accurate grid.

2 Place the paper under the presser foot and lower your needle onto the first $1/4''$ (6 mm) line from the right edge of your paper.

3 Place a piece of masking tape on the throat plate right next to the edge of the paper.

4 Remove the paper. The edge of the masking tape can now serve as a $1/4''$ (6 mm) guide.

The Presser Foot

Most sewing machines come with a presser foot that is the proper width to easily sew $1/4''$ (6 mm) seam allowances by lining up the raw edges against the side of the presser foot. To test your presser foot, simply line up the edge of a scrap of fabric with the right edge of you presser foot. Stitch down the edge of the fabric, then take a ruler or tape measure and measure the seam allowance.

If you don't have a $1/4''$ (6 mm) presser foot you can purchase a patchwork presser foot for your machine, which will make sewing for patchwork and quilting easier.

Sewing a Corner

1 About 1" (2.5 cm) before you reach the corner, stop stitching with the needle still down, then shorten the stitch length setting on your machine to about 15–20 stitches per inch (1–1.5 mm; this will reinforce your corner). Continue stitching until you are $1/4''$ (6 mm) from the edge.

2 When you are $1/4''$ (6 mm) from the edge of the fabric, stop sewing with the needle down in the fabric, lift the presser foot and pivot the fabric so that the adjoining edge is now vertical in front of you. Lower the presser foot.

3 Sew for about 1" (2.5 cm), then stop stitching (with the needle still down) and return your stitch length to the regular setting (10–12 stitches per inch [2.5–3 mm]), then continue stitching.

4 Repeat Steps 1–3 for each corner, then remove the fabric from the machine and clip the corners (p. 157) before turning the piece right side out.

Sewing a Curve

1 When your seam begins to curve, stop sewing, with your needle still down, and shorten the stitch length on your machine to about 15 stitches per inch (1.5 mm).

2 Stitch slowly around the curve as you guide the fabric with your hands, keeping your seam allowances constant. Going slowly will give you better control to keep your stitching smooth and even.

3 Once you have finished sewing the curve, stop stitching (with the needle still down) and return your stitch length to the regular setting (10–12 stitches per inch [2.5–3 mm]), then continue stitching.

4 Once you are done stitching, remove the fabric from the machine and clip the curves before turning the piece right side out.

Creating Hems with Mitered Corners

Mitering is a really lovely finishing technique used on corners to create a nice and neat 45-degree angle.

1 Fold the raw edges to be hemmed over ½" (1.3 cm), toward the wrong side, and press. Fold over another ½" (1.3 cm) and press again.

2 Unfold the edges and clip the corners near the outer crease lines (**figure 1**). Then, fold the clipped corners over ½" (1.3 cm), toward the wrong side, and press (**figure 2**).

3 Fold the edges again along the existing crease lines, forming the miters at each corner.

4 Topstitch (p. 155) around the hem or handstitch the hem in place with a blindstitch (p. 156).

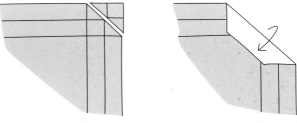

figure 1   figure 2

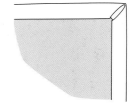

figure 3

Patchwork Binding

Patchwork binding is a great way to use up fabric scraps because you can piece the binding together, using small scraps (they'll need to be at least 2" [5 cm] wide but can be varying lengths). Before you begin cutting your fabric for binding, you need to determine the total length of binding you'll need for your project. Measure the length on all four sides of your project and add them together, then add about 12" (30.5 cm) for finishing the binding. The following instructions will create ½" (1.3 cm) wide finished binding.

1 Square up your fabric (p. 14) and cut enough 2" (5 cm) wide strips to equal the length you need, the strips can be various lengths and prints/colors because you are creating patchwork binding. Remember that you will need seam allowance so you'll want to account for a little extra length when cutting your strips.

2 Place 2 of the binding strips right sides together, placing them end to end to form an L shape. Then, stitch the 2 strips together diagonally and trim the seam allowances to ¼" (6 mm; **figure 1**).

3 Open up the strips so they are lying flat and press the seam allowances open.

4 Repeat Steps 2 and 3 until you've stitched all of your strips together, forming one long strip of fabric.

5 Fold the strip in half lengthwise with wrong sides together and press. Then, unfold the strip and fold over each long edge, toward the wrong side, by ½" (1.3 cm) so that the raw edges meet at the center crease; press (**figure 2**).

6 Refold the binding along the center crease, enclosing the raw edges, and press again (**figure 3**).

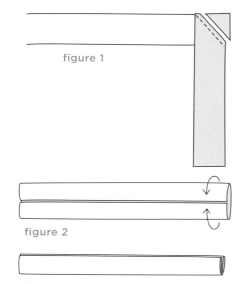

figure 1

figure 2

figure 3

Attach Binding with Mitered Corners

1 Unfold the binding completely and then fold under one short end of the binding strip, toward the wrong side by 1″ (2.5 cm) or as directed by the pattern, and press.

2 Starting from the bottom center of the project (with the right side facing up), place the folded-under end of the binding on top of the project, lining up the raw edge of the binding with the raw edge of the project (right sides will be together); pin in place to the first corner.

3 Start sewing the binding to the project along the first crease (closest to the raw edge), about 2″ (5 cm) from the folded-under edge, through all layers.

4 Stop stitching about ¼″ (6 mm) from the first corner and backtack (p. 154; for extra security you can backtack twice).

5 To form a mitered corner, rotate the project 90 degrees so that the adjoining edge of the project is now vertical in front of you. Fold the binding fabric up, away from the project, at a 45-degree angle (**figure 1**).

6 Fold the binding back down along the raw edge of the project, aligning the raw edges as before. Stitch the binding along this edge, as in Step 3, beginning at the top edge of the fabric and sewing until you are ¼″ (6 mm) away from the next corner (**figure 2**).

7 Repeat Steps 3–6 to bind the remaining edges and miter the corners. When you reach your starting point, overlap the folded-under edge by about 1″ (2.5 cm) or as directed by the pattern, and then trim the binding if necessary. Continue stitching until you have reached the beginning of your stitch line.

8 Refold the binding along the bottom crease and then fold the binding over the edge of the project from front to back, placing the folded-under edge on the back of the project (it should be directly across from the bottom of the binding on the opposite side and should cover the stitches). Handstitch the binding to the back of the project using a slip stitch (p. 156); make sure to cover the machine stitches and fold each corner into a miter as before.

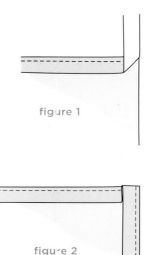

figure 1

figure 2

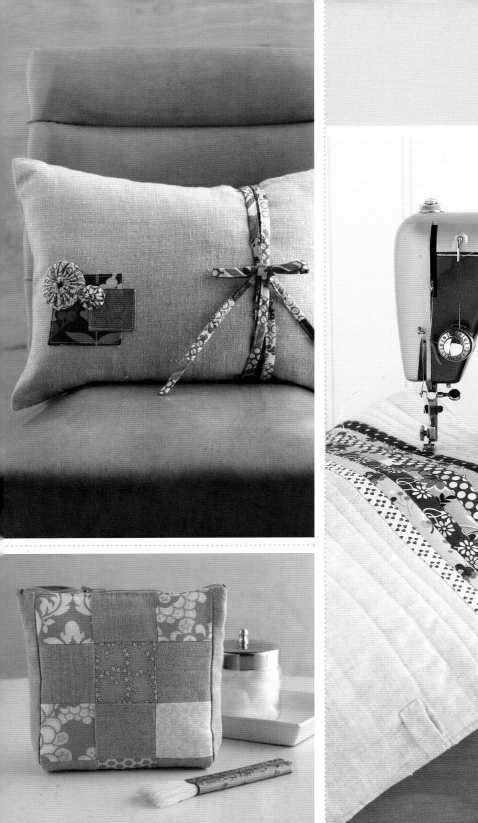

the projects

Sprucing up your home with simple and practical hand-made items is what gives Zakka its charm. The items in this book are easy to create and will brighten up any room in an instant! Create the pretty *Appliquéd Pillow* (p. 86) to accent your living room furniture, or the cute *Button Calendar* (p. 102) for a reusable alternative to store-bought calendars. Outfit your kitchen with the lovely, and useful, *Kitchen Towel* (p. 134) or accessorize your dining table with the clever *Placemat and Napkin Set* (p. 74). Any of the projects in this book would also make a lovely gift for a treasured family member or friend, so you might want to make two (or three) of each in different colors! The possibilities are endless when you begin to use your fabric stash and your creativity to brighten up your home or to create special one-of-a-kind gifts.

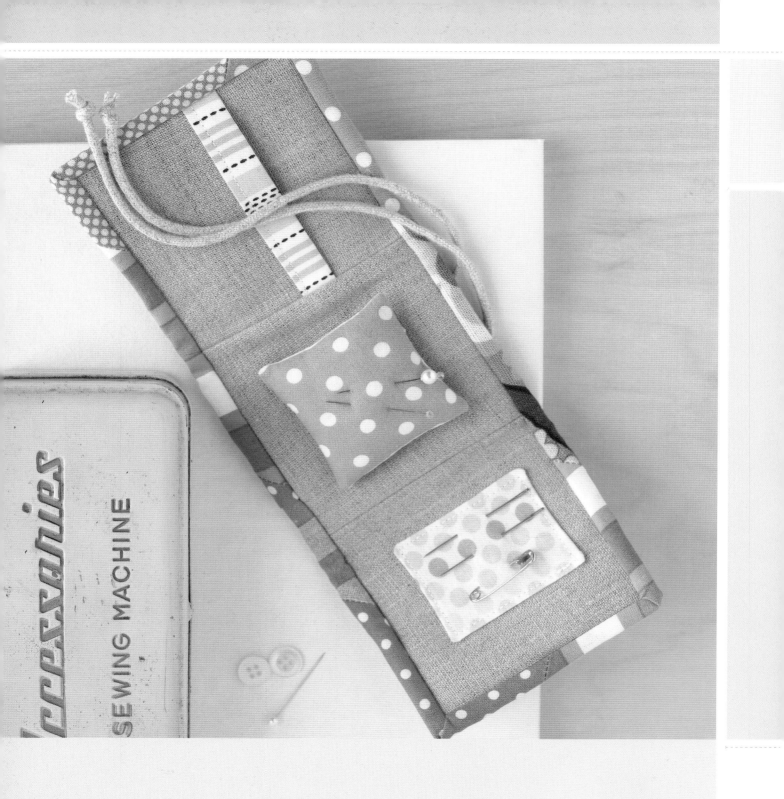

finished size

9½" (24 cm) wide x 3½" (9 cm) long when open. About 3" (7.5 cm) wide x 3½" (9 cm) long when closed)

materials

Linen *(shown: natural)*

1 rectangle measuring 9½" x 3½" (24 x 9 cm) for shell

3 squares, each measuring 3½" x 3½" (9 x 9 cm) for inside panels

1 rectangle measuring 3½" x 2¼" (9 x 5.5 cm) for interior pocket

Various cotton prints *(3 different prints shown)*

1 strip measuring 2" x 3½" (5 x 9 cm) for pocket accent

2 squares, each measuring 2½" x 2½" (6.5 x 6.5 cm) for pincushion

1 rectangle measuring 2" x 2½" (5 x 6.5 cm) for needle panel

Low-loft batting

9½" x 3½" (24 x 9 cm) rectangle

About 38" (96.5 cm) of patch-work binding (see p. 20)

Scrap of light interfacing, at least 2" x 2½" (5 x 6.5 cm)

Small amount of fiberfill

About 20" (51 cm) of cotton cording

tools

Blunt pencil or small knitting needle (optional)

Walking foot for sewing machine (optional)

travel SEWING KIT

Having a needle, thread, and pins handy while on-the-go is easy with this travel sewing kit. It folds up neatly and is small enough to fit in almost any purse or handbag. This convenient and compact little kit is perfect to make for yourself or to give as a gift to a pal who loves to sew.

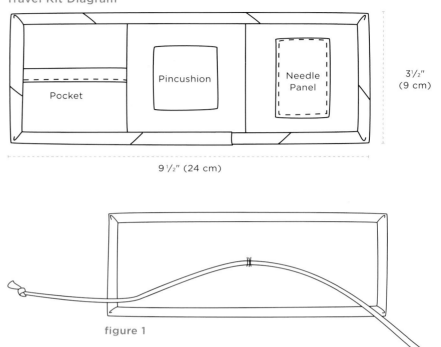

Travel Kit Diagram

Pocket

Pincushion

Needle Panel

3½" (9 cm)

9½" (24 cm)

figure 1

Travel Sewing Kit

Note: All seam allowances are ¼" (6 mm) unless otherwise indicated.

CREATE THE POCKET

1 On the pocket accent, fold each short edge over to the wrong side ½" (1.3 cm), then fold the piece in half lengthwise, enclosing the raw edges, with wrong sides together so that you have a piece measuring 3½" x ½" (9 x 1.3 cm); press. This will be used to bind the edge of the pocket.

2 Place the binding (made in Step 1) over one 3½" (9 cm) edge of the interior pocket so that the raw edge is encased inside the binding.

3 Edgestitch (p. 154) along the bottom of the binding (see diagram at top right for assistance).

4 With one of inside panels facing right side up, place the pocket on top, right side up. Line up the bottom raw edge of the pocket with one raw edge of the inside panel; pin in place (see the diagram).

MAKE THE PINCUSHION

5 Place the 2 pincushion pieces right sides together and line up the edges.

6 Leaving a small opening for turning, stitch around the perimeter of the square. Clip the corners (p. 157), then turn right side out through the opening. Push out the corners (you'll probably need to use a blunt pencil or small knitting needle to do this; a point turner may be too large to maneuver easily) and then press.

7 Stuff the pincushion with fiberfill; you'll want to stuff it until it is pretty firm, but be careful not to overstuff.

8 Turn in the seam allowances at the opening by ¼" (6 mm) and finger press (p. 154), then handstitch closed with a slip stitch (p. 156). Set aside.

MAKE THE NEEDLE PANEL

9 Pin the needle panel piece right side down on top of the light interfacing. Stitch together around the edges of the needle panel piece ¼" (6 mm) from the edge.

10 If necessary, trim the interfacing even with the edges of the needle panel piece, then clip the corners.

11 Cut a small opening in the interfacing only and turn the piece right side out through the opening. Gently push out the corners as in Step 6 and press; set aside.

MAKE THE INTERIOR

12 Create 1 long interior piece by stitching the 3 inside panels together, placing the panel with the pocket at one edge (see diagram at left). Make sure the pocket accent faces up and the seam to connect the interior panels runs along one side of the pocket. Press the seam allowances open.

13 Take the pincushion you made in Steps 5–8 and center it over the middle panel of the interior piece just made; pin in place. With needle and thread, handstitch the pin cushion to the linen using a blindstitch, placing your stitches underneath the pincushion by about $1/4$–$1/2''$ (6 mm–1.3 cm) rather than right at the edge. Tie off the thread and clip the thread tails.

14 Next, take the needle panel you made in Steps 9–11 and center it over the remaining empty end panel (opposite the end panel with the pocket). Pin in place. Edgestitch around the needle panel.

ASSEMBLE AND BIND THE LAYERS

15 Layer the pieces in the following order: linen shell (right side down), batting, interior panel (right side up). Pin together, placing the pins at least $3/4''$ (2 cm) from the edge.

16 Unfold the patchwork binding and fold under the raw edge at one end $1/4''$ (6 mm); finger press. Bind the edges and miter the corners, according to the instructions under Attach Binding with Mitered Corners on p. 21. When you reach your starting point, overlap the folded-under edge of the binding by about $1/2''$ (1.3 cm). Use the walking foot to sew the binding if desired.

FINISH THE KIT

17 Fold the cotton cording in half to find the center point and then lay this point down at the center of the outside of the sewing kit.

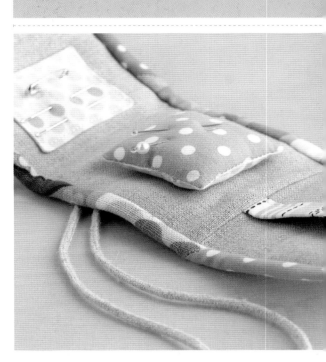

18 Tack the cording directly to the center of the sewing kit with a whipstitch (p. 157), sewing only through the linen shell (**figure 1**).

19 To use the sewing kit, simply stick some pins into the pincushion, insert a few needles through the needle panel and use the pocket to hold any other little bits and pieces you might need. Now, fold up the kit, tie the cording, and you're ready to go!

About 19" (48.5 cm) in circumference

Linen *(shown: natural)*

20 scraps, each at least 3" x 3" (8 x 8 cm)

Various cotton prints *(12 different prints shown)*

12 scraps, each at least 4" x 4" (10 x 10 cm)

Paper or card stock for templates

Fiberfill for stuffing

Triangle and Pentagon templates (p. 150)

Copy machine (optional)

patchwork BALL

This adorable little patchwork ball is the perfect addition to any nursery. Soft and plush with bright, colorful shapes completely handpieced by you, this is sure to delight any precious tot in your life. You may find yourself making a whole set in a variety of colors for your little one to enjoy.

Patchwork Ball

PREPARE SHAPES

1 Copy or trace the Triangle and Pentagon templates onto paper or card stock (card stock makes a sturdier template), then add ¼" (6 mm) seam allowances to each. Cut out the templates and set aside (these will be used to cut out the fabric shapes). Using the original templates (without seam allowances added), copy or trace the templates onto paper (I suggest using paper for these, rather than card stock) until you have 20 triangle templates and 12 pentagon templates. Cut out all templates and set aside (these will be used for English Paper Piecing in Steps 4–8).

2 Using the triangle template with seam allowances, pin the template to the wrong side of one of the linen scraps (be sure to place the triangle on the straight grain [p. 154]) and trace around the template. Cut out the triangle. Repeat entire step nineteen times so that you have a total of 20 linen triangles.

3 Repeat Step 2, using the pentagon template (with seam allowances) and pinning it to the wrong side of a cotton print scrap, until you have a total of 12 cotton pentagons.

PIECE THE TRIANGLES

4 Pin a triangle template (without seam allowances) to the center of the wrong side of one of your linen triangles so that the ¼" (6 mm) seam allowances of the fabric surround the paper template (**figure 1**). Fold

TIP

This project uses English Paper Piecing to prepare the fabric shapes for the ball. You can read about this technique on p. 120, but this project requires specific folding methods that are explained in the instructions, along with illustrations.

each corner of the fabric triangle over the template so that the point of the template lies in the crease of the fold (**figure 2**). Next, fold the ¼" (6 mm) seam allowance of one side of the fabric triangle over the template (**figure 3**).

5 Fold the two remaining sides of the fabric triangle over the template, creating crisp corners. With a handsewing needle and thread, whipstitch (p. 157) the corners together with a few stitches, being careful not to sew the fabric to the template (**figure 4**). Remove the pin.

6 Repeat Steps 3 and 4 with the nineteen remaining triangles.

PIECE THE PENTAGONS

7 Pin a pentagon template to the center of the wrong side of one of your cotton pentagons so that the ¼" (6 mm) seam allowances of the fabric surround the paper template as in Step 4. Fold the ¼" (6 mm) seam allowance of one side of the fabric pentagon over the template (**figure 5**).

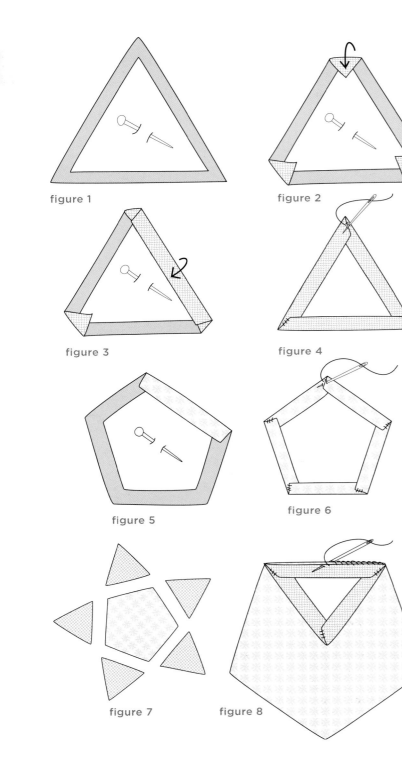

figure 1

figure 2

figure 3

figure 4

figure 5

figure 6

figure 7

figure 8

8 Continue folding each side of the fabric pentagon over the template until all edges are folded over. With a handsewing needle and thread, whipstitch the seam allowances together at each point of the pentagon with a few stitches, being careful not to sew the fabric to the template (**figure 6**). Remove the pin.

9 Repeat Steps 6 and 7 with the 11 remaining pentagons.

HANDSTITCH THE SHAPES TOGETHER

10 Create a star shape by sewing 5 triangles to one of the pentagons (**figure 7**) in the following manner: place 1 triangle right sides together with 1 pentagon, lining up one edge of the triangle with one edge of the pentagon. With a handsewing needle and thread, whipstitch the pieces together along the matched edge, picking up only two or three threads of the fabric so that your stitching remains as close to the edge as possible. Be careful not to sew through the paper template (**figure 8**). Continue in this manner until all five edges of the pentagon are attached to a triangle. Repeat entire step to create a second star shape; set aside one of the completed star shapes.

11 Now you will attach 5 pentagons to one of the star shapes using the technique described in Step 10 to attach them. See **figure 9** for the placement of the pentagons.

12 Now attach 1 triangle to each of the pentagons attached to the star in Step 11.

31

Use the technique described in Step 10 to attach them and see **figure 10** for placement of the triangles.

13 Whipstitch the edges together as shown in **figure 11a**, following the arrows to attach the indicated edges to each other. Use the technique described in Step 10 to stitch the edges together, folding as necessary to place right sides together and then stitching as before. This will form a bowl shape (**figure 11b**); set aside.

14 Repeat Steps 11–13 with the second star shape (created in Step 10) and the remaining shapes to form a second bowl shape.

15 Handstitch the bowl shapes together (with right sides facing out) using whipstitch and holding the edges together as you stitch, being careful to keep the stitching as close to the edge as possible without stitching through the paper, as before. Leave an opening large enough to turn and stuff the ball (**figure 12**).

16 Turn the ball inside out and remove all of the paper templates, then turn the ball right side out and firmly stuff with the fiberfill. Whipstitch the opening closed and you're done!

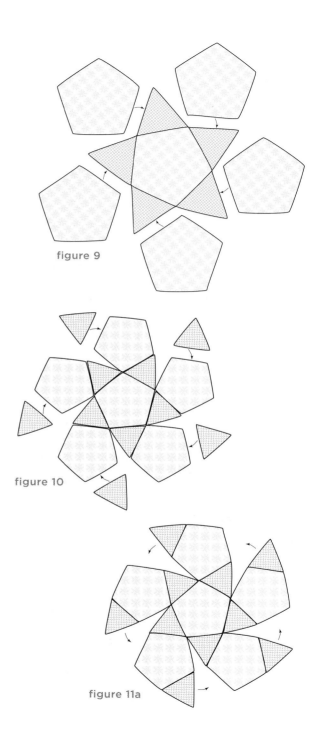

figure 9

figure 10

figure 11a

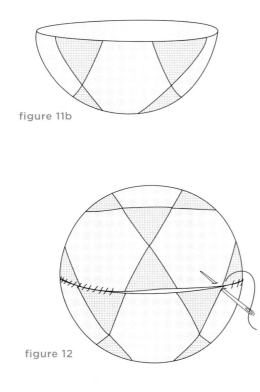

figure 11b

figure 12

finished size

7" (18 cm) wide x 6" (15 cm)
long x 2" (5 cm) deep (front to
back)

materials

Linen *(shown: natural)*
  10 squares, each $2\frac{1}{2}$" x $2\frac{1}{2}$"
  (6.5 x 6.5 cm) for shell

  2 strips, each $1\frac{1}{4}$" x $14\frac{1}{2}$"
  (3.2 x 37 cm) for shell

Various cotton prints *(11 different prints shown)*
  11 squares, each $2\frac{1}{2}$" x $2\frac{1}{2}$"
  (6.5 x 6.5 cm) for shell

  8" x $14\frac{1}{2}$" (20.5 x 37 cm [use
  1 of the prints already used])
  rectangle for lining

Fusible fleece
  6" x $13\frac{3}{4}$" (15 x 35 cm)
  rectangle

7" (18 cm) standard zipper

tools

Zipper foot for sewing machine
Point turner (optional)

cosmetics POUCH

I'm a bag lady. I have a little pouch for just about everything. I got it from my mother who's far worse than I, so you could say my mother inspired me to make this bag. The pouch is made with the popular and easy-to-make Nine-Patch quilt block. Combining the linen blocks with cotton prints in a carefully chosen color palette make this simple pouch a stunning statement.

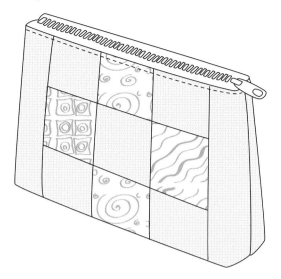

Cosmetics Pouch

Note: All seam allowances are ¼″ (6 mm) unless otherwise indicated.

CREATE THE SHELL

1 Lay out your cotton and linen squares in the order you would like them to be by placing them on a table in front of you in rows of three, alternating linen and cotton squares for a checkerboard effect (**figure 1**). This will give you the chance to arrange your squares as desired before sewing (you should have twenty-one squares).

2 Begin stitching the first row of squares together by placing 2 squares with right sides together, matching up all edges; pin and then stitch along one edge. Add another square in the same manner to create a row. You will now have a piece measuring 2½″ x 6½″ (5 x 16.5 cm). Press all seam allowances to one side. Repeat entire step for the next 3-square row, pressing all seam allowances in the opposite direction from the first row. Repeat entire step for all subsequent rows, alternating the direction in which you press the seam allowances on each row. You will have a total of seven rows of 3 squares each.

3 Now stitch the first two rows together, placing them right sides together and lining up all seams and edges. Pin together along the top 6½″ (16.5 cm) edge and then stitch together along the pinned edge; press the seam allowances up toward Row 1. Repeat entire step to stitch together Rows 3 and 4, then Rows 5 and 6, leaving Row 7 free.

4 Stitch each unit together in order (stitch Row 2 to Row 3 and Row 4 to Row 5) along the 6½″ (16.5 cm) edge, pressing the seam allowances down. Stitch Row 7 to Row 6 in the same manner and press the seam allowances down.

5 Lay the patchwork unit just created on the table in front of you, right side up. Lay the linen strips on top at each side, aligning and pinning the 14½″ (37 cm) edges. Stitch together along the pinned edges. Press the seam allowances toward the linen.

figure 1

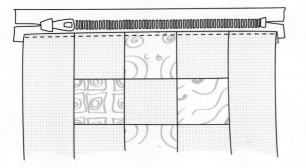

figure 2

6 Turn the patchwork unit over (right side down) and center the fusible fleece on top, fusible side down. Fuse the fleece according to the manufacturer's instructions.

ATTACH THE ZIPPER AND FINISH THE SHELL

7 Fold over each short (8″ [20.5 cm]) edge of the patchwork unit ¼″ (6 mm), toward the wrong side, and press. Close your zipper and lay it on the table right side up. Lay one of the folded edges of the patchwork unit, right side up, on top of one side of the zipper tape, ¼″ (6 mm) from the zipper teeth; pin in place (make sure the top of the zipper pull lies ½″ [1.3 cm] below the raw edge at the side of the patchwork unit). With the zipper foot on the sewing machine, edgestitching (p. 154) along the edge of the patchwork unit (**figure 2**).

8 Lay the opposite folded-under edge of the patchwork unit, right side up, on the opposite side of the zipper tape. Pin as in Step 7 (you now have a tube of fabric). This is where it gets a little tricky—just be patient and stitch slowly. Unzip the zipper (this will make stitching easier) and stitch as in Step 7; you'll find that you have to turn the end of the pouch partially inside out to stitch all the way to the end of the zipper. Be sure to keep the rest of the pouch fabric out of the way as you stitch to the end of the zipper. Leave the needle down to proceed to the next step.

9 Pivot the pouch so that the zipper is now horizontal in front of you (you may want to close the zipper at this point to make stitching easier). Make sure the pouch fabric is out of the way and then slowly stitch across the zipper tapes, close to the edge, to secure completely to the linen. Repeat at the opposite end of the zipper to secure the zipper tape edges.

10 Once you've finished inserting the zipper, turn the pouch completely inside out (make sure your zipper is still open!). Lay the pouch flat, aligning the side seams and pinning them together. Put your regular presser foot back on the sewing machine and sew the side seams. Press the side seams open.

11 Flatten one side seam of the pouch on the table so that it lies directly down the center, forming a point at the corner. Using the acrylic ruler and fabric marking pen or tailor's chalk, measure about 1" (2.5 cm) down from the corner and mark, then draw a line across the corner (perpendicular to the side seam) through the mark (**figure 3**). Stitch along this line, then clip off the corner of the fabric about $1/4$" (6 mm) below the stitch line (**figure 4**). Repeat entire step for the opposite corner.

CREATE AND ATTACH THE LINING

12 Fold the cotton lining piece (8" x 14$1/2$" [20.5 x 37 cm]) in half widthwise, right sides together, lining up the edges. Pin and then stitch the side seams. Repeat Step 11 to square the corners. Turn the lining right side out.

13 With the shell inside out, pull the lining up around the pouch (wrong sides will be together). Fold in the seam allowance at

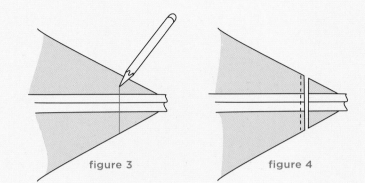

figure 3

figure 4

the top of the lining pouch and press. The folded edge of the lining should be on top of the zipper tape, in line with the shell edge (on the other side of the zipper tape).

14 With the needle and thread, handsew the lining to the zipper tape with a slip stitch (p. 156), being careful not to stitch through the shell fabric. Turn the pouch right side out and push out the corners (use the point turner if necessary). Now you're ready to fill your pouch and go!

Doll is about 17½" (44.5 cm) tall x about 17" (43 cm) wide, from tip of hand to tip of hand, across chest. Finished dress is 7" (18 cm) long x 10" (25.5 cm) wide (at the gathered waist; the dress can be adjusted to fit, if necessary, with the placement of button and buttonhole—see Steps 40–45 on p. 49).

materials

Linen *(shown: natural)*
1 fat quarter for lamb and dress waistband

Faux Sherpa fleece
¼ yd (23 cm) for lamb

Various cotton prints
(16 different prints shown; see notes on p. 42)
10 squares, each 2½" x 2½" (6.5 x 6.5 cm; mark A)

8 strips, each 2½" x 7½" (6.5 x 19 cm; mark B)

4 rectangles, each 2½" x 3½" (6.5 x 9 cm; mark C)

4 rectangles, each 2½" x 3" (6.5 x 7.5 cm; mark D)

4 rectangles, each 2½" x 2" (6.5 x 5 cm; mark E)

2 rectangles, each 2½" x ½" (6.5 x 11.5 cm; mark F)

Fiberfill for stuffing

Yarn for pom-poms
(shown: yellow)

Embroidery floss in various colors for face *(shown: black, white, and pink)*

⅝" (1.5 cm) button *(shown: wooden flower-shaped button)*

Paper or card stock for patterns

Cardboard for templates

Powder blush (optional) for lamb face

CONTINUED ON NEXT PAGE

little lamb SOFTIE

I made this sweet lamb for my daughter when she was a baby, and she loved it. She especially liked the way the linen hands and feet felt on her gums when she was teething. The cheerful patchwork skirt and happy little face will make this doll a delightful companion for the special little girl in your life. My daughter still loves her little lamb, and I hope that she will continue to treasure it for years to come.

TIP

The crosswise grain of the faux Sherpa fleece fabric is very stretchy so be sure to follow the grainlines (p. 154) on your patterns (which are all lengthwise grainlines). The fabric pile should also be taken into account, so be sure to cut the pattern pieces from one layer of the fabric, not doubled. This will allow you to cut more accurately.

Little Lamb Softie

Notes: All seam allowances are ¼″ (6 mm) unless otherwise indicated.

+ Be sure to mark the cotton prints as indicated in the Materials list on p. 41, using a water-soluble fabric pen or tailor's chalk to label each piece on the wrong side for easy identification when assembling the patchwork dress.

+ See the sidebar on p. 44 for definitions of pattern markings.

+ When instructed to "cut reverse," flip the pattern piece over to the back side to cut. This is done to create pieces that are mirror images of each other.

+ To ensure that the fabric on the patchwork dress (see Steps 30–36 on pp. 47 and 48) does not ravel, sew the patchwork pieces together with a serger or the zigzag stitch on your sewing machine (if your sewing machine has an overlock stitch function, this can also be

used). If using a serger, be sure to set the stitch width to 6 mm; if using a zigzag stitch, be sure that the fabric is placed so that the left swing of the needle is ¼″ (6 mm) from the raw edge (you can trim the seam allowances closer to the zigzag stitch line if necessary). Refer to your sewing machine manual for more information on using the zigzag (or overlock) stitch function.

CUT THE FABRIC

1 Trace each pattern piece onto paper or card stock and cut out. Then, cut the following pieces as indicated. You can either pin the pattern pieces to the wrong side of the fabric and then cut around them, or trace them onto the fabric (wrong side) with a water-soluble fabric pen or tailor's chalk and then cut them out along the traced lines. Label each piece on the wrong side with a fabric pen or tailor's chalk for easy identification.

FROM FAUX FLEECE:

- 2 Head Back (cut 1, cut 1 reverse)
- 4 Tail/Ears
- 2 Head Front (cut 1, cut 1 reverse)
- 4 Legs
- 4 Arms
- 4 Body Front/Back (cut 2, cut 2 reverse)

FROM LINEN:

- 1 Face
- 8 Hand/Foot
- 2 Tail/Ears
- 1 rectangle, 10½" x 3" (26.5 x 7.5 cm) for patchwork dress waistband

ASSEMBLE THE LEGS AND ARMS

2 Place 1 Hand/Foot piece right sides together with 1 Leg piece, aligning the straight edge of the Hand/Foot with one short edge of the Leg and pin. Stitch together and then finger press (p. 154) the seam allowances toward the fleece. Repeat entire step to attach one Hand/Foot to each of the remaining Legs, then attach one Hand/Foot to each Arm as well.

3 Place 2 of the Foot/Leg pieces right sides together, matching up all of the edges. Sew together, leaving the top (flat fleece) edge open for stuffing. Repeat to sew together the remaining Foot/Leg pieces, then repeat to sew together the Hand/Arm pieces. Clip the curves (p. 157) on each piece and then turn inside out.

4 Stuff the arms and legs with fiberfill. Stuff them quite well, but not too firmly. Leave about ½" (1.3 cm) at the top of each piece free of stuffing. Set aside.

ASSEMBLING THE EARS AND TAIL

5 Place 1 linen and 1 fleece Ear/Tail right sides together and pin. Stitch them together, leaving the flat side open. You don't need to clip the curves on these because the fleece is stretchy. Turn right side out. Repeat entire step with the remaining linen and 1 fleece Ear/Tail. Then repeat to create the tail with the remaining fleece Ear/Tail pieces. Set aside.

ASSEMBLING THE HEAD

6 Pin the 2 Head Front pieces right sides together. Stitch them together at the top of head only (short edges; see pattern). Open up the seamed Head Front piece and finger press the seam allowances open.

7 Pin the Head Front piece and the Face piece right sides together; start by pinning the seam of the Head Front piece to the center notch of the Face piece, then pin each edge of the Head Front piece to the edges of the face at the dart, matching the notches, and then ease in (see the sidebar on p. 44) and pin the remaining fabric (**figure 1**).

8 Stitch around the pinned edge (don't forget to remove the pins as you go; see the sidebar for tips on sewing this seam). Flip up the Head Front piece and finger press the seam allowances toward the fleece (clip the curves if necessary so that the seam lies neatly).

9 Fold the face in half with right sides together, matching up the edges of the dart. Stitch the dart from the bottom edge of the fleece to the dart point as shown in **figure 2**; when you are about ¼" (6 mm) from the dart point, set the stitch length on your machine to 2 mm and finish sewing the dart (this will reinforce the tip of the dart). Do not backtack (p. 154), instead, clip the threads leaving tails several inches long. Tie the thread tails securely and leave about 1" (2.5 cm) tails (**figure 2**). You have now created the lamb face (the tip of the dart will become the nose).

10 Place the 2 Head Back pieces right sides together lining up the edges and pin together along the straight (notched) raw

easing in

When a pattern instructs you to "ease" or "ease in" fabric, you are attaching a longer section to a shorter section and/or attaching opposing curves to create a shaped seam as in the Little Lamb Softie. You want to attach the two pieces as smoothly as possible without catching tucks or gathers in the seam. To do this, first pin together the two pieces evenly at the ends and/or at the indicated notches, then, continue to pin the area in between, making sure the raw edges match up smoothly. This will require you to force the extra fabric away from the edge and into the fabric below the seam allowance. After you place each pin, allow the fabric to bubble slightly, then, while holding the edges even, gently work the extra fabric back, away from the edge by smoothing it back, then place another pin to hold it in place. It may also be necessary to gently stretch one of the pieces to accommodate the other, but don't stretch too harshly because you don't want to warp the fabric or the shape of the seam. The closer you place the pins, the easier it will be to sew the seam without catching tucks or gathers.

When sewing the seam, go very slowly, smoothing the fabric as necessary to keep the excess away from the edge. It may be necessary to adjust as you sew by leaving the needle down and raising the presser foot to smooth the fabric or realign the edges.

USING THE PATTERN:

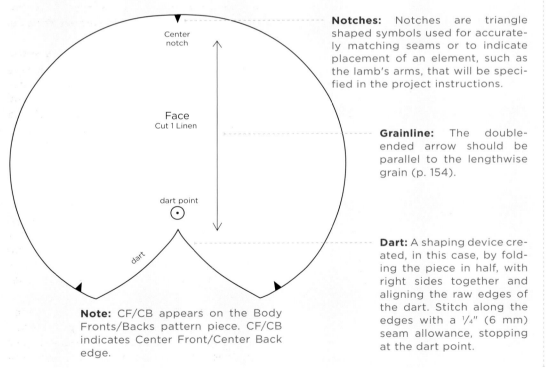

Center notch

Face
Cut 1 Linen

dart point

dart

Note: CF/CB appears on the Body Fronts/Backs pattern piece. CF/CB indicates Center Front/Center Back edge.

Notches: Notches are triangle shaped symbols used for accurately matching seams or to indicate placement of an element, such as the lamb's arms, that will be specified in the project instructions.

Grainline: The double-ended arrow should be parallel to the lengthwise grain (p. 154).

Dart: A shaping device created, in this case, by folding the piece in half, with right sides together and aligning the raw edges of the dart. Stitch along the edges with a ¼" (6 mm) seam allowance, stopping at the dart point.

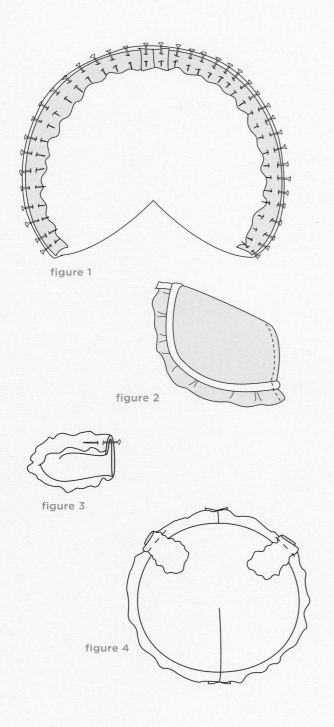

figure 1

figure 2

figure 3

figure 4

edges only. Stitch the straight edges, then open up the piece and finger press the seam allowances open. Set aside for now.

11 Take the linen/fleece ears you made earlier and fold each almost in half, toward the linen (be sure to fold the ears in the opposite direction so that they will be mirror images of each other when placed on the head. Pin to hold in place (**figure 3**).

12 Place the lamb face flat and right side up in front of you. Place 1 ear on each side of the head, with the top (folded) edge of the ear at the notch. Be sure that right sides are together (linen to linen). Allow the raw edges of the ears to hang past the raw edge of the lamb face by about ¼" (6 mm) and pin in place. Check that the ears are level so that they don't end up lopsided; use the edge of your acrylic ruler to check that the ears are directly across from each other. Hand-baste (p. 154) each ear in place, about ⅛" (3 mm) from the edge of the lamb face and remove the pins (**figure 4**).

13 Now place the Head Back on top of the lamb face with right sides together (make sure that the ears are sandwiched in between), matching up the edges, and pin. Stitch all the way around, through all the layers, leaving the bottom neck edge open. Turn right side out and set aside. You have now created the lamb head.

ASSEMBLE THE BODY

14 Place 2 of the Body Front/Back pieces right sides together, matching up the edges and notches; pin along the straight CF/CB edge. Sew together along the pinned edge (don't forget to remove the pins as you go!). This is now the body front; set aside.

15 Take the fleece tail you made earlier, fold it in half lengthwise, and pin. Place 1 of the remaining Body Front/Back pieces right side up and place the folded edge of the tail at the bottom notch (farthest from the neck edge). Allow the raw edge of the tail to hang past the raw edge of the Body piece by about 1/4" (6 mm). Hand-baste the tail in place about 1/8" (3 mm) from the Body raw edge. Then, place the last Body Front/Back piece on top, right side down, matching and pinning the straight CF/CB edges as before. Make sure that the tail is sandwiched in between the layers and then sew along the pinned edge, beginning at the bottom edge and sewing only to the top notch (be sure to backtack) This is now the body back.

16 Place the body back and body front right sides together; pin and then stitch at the shoulders only.

17 With the lamb head right side out and the body still inside out, place the head inside the body, between the shoulders, so that the right sides are together; match up the neck edge and pin. Stitch around the neck edge. Push the head up, out of the body so that it is inside out.

18 Flip the back of the body up, over the head. *Then, position 1 arm at the notch below each shoulder (the top of the arm will be at the notch), with the arms lying on top of the body front, and allowing the raw edges of the arms to hang past the raw edge of the body by about 1/4" (6 mm). Hand-baste each arm to the body, about 1/8" (3 mm) from the edge of the body. Repeat from * to position 1 leg at each notch on the bottom edge (the outside of the leg should be at the notch). Flip the back body down over the front body and the arms and legs.

19 Pin the front and back body together around the edge, ensuring that the arms and legs are sandwiched in between the layers and are kept out of the way of the needle when sewing. The arms and legs are long so you will probably have to fold them to keep them between the layers. Stitch around the body, then turn the lamb right side out, passing the arms, legs, and head through the opening at the back. Remove any visible basting stitches.

20 Stuff the head and the body with fiberfill. Handstitch the back opening closed tightly with a whipstitch (p. 157) and be sure to knot the thread very securely.

MAKE AND ATTACH THE POM-POMS

21 Trace and then cut out two of the Pompom template from cardboard. Place the two templates together and begin wrapping your yarn tightly around them (**figure 5**). The more yarn you use and the tighter you wrap, the denser your pom-pom will be.

22 Holding the wrapped templates firmly between your fingers, slip your scissors between the 2 cardboard templates (**figure 6**) and carefully cut the yarn all the way around the edge, keeping your scissors between the 2 templates the whole way.

23 Take a long piece of yarn and slip it between the 2 templates (you are still holding the cut yarns in place with your fingers) and tie it once or twice tightly around all the strands of yarn, between the 2 templates (**figure 7**).

24 You can now remove the templates as all the strands of yarn should be firmly tied together around the middle. Trim the tips of the yarns to make the pom-pom nice and even.

25 Now tie the yarn tails of one pom-pom around each of the ears on the lamb doll, near the head (see **figure 8**). Conceal the knot underneath the pom-pom and clip the yarn tails.

CREATE THE LAMB FACE

See **figure 8** for assistance with the following steps.

26 Using several strands of embroidery floss (shown: black), create 1 eye on each side of the tip of the dart on the lamb's face

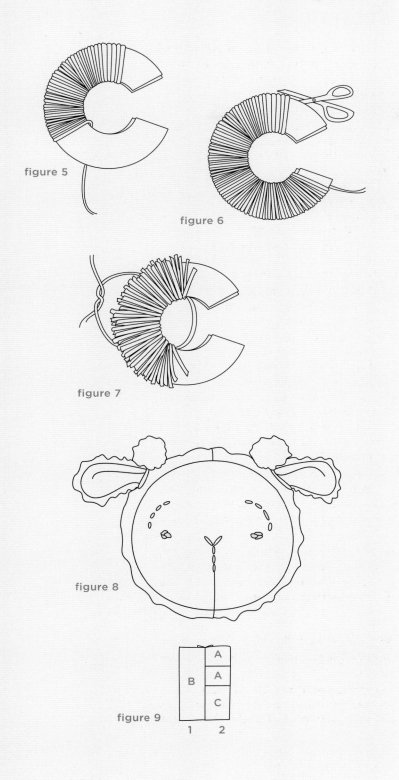

figure 5

figure 6

figure 7

figure 8

figure 9

1   2

with French knots (p. 156). You can add eyelashes by using one strand of embroidery floss to make three running stitches along one side of each eye.

27 Using one or two strands of embroidery floss (shown: pink), create a nose with running stitches (p. 157) directly over the point of the dart and along the dart seam line; use two long diagonal running stitches at the top to create a V shape, then use smaller running stitches underneath, along the dart seam line.

28 Using one or two strands of embroidery floss (shown: white), create an eyebrow over each eye with a running stitch.

29 If you'd like, you can add a light layer of blush to give her rosy cheeks; use your fingertips to add the blush under the eyes, gently rubbing it onto the face in a circular motion.

CREATE THE PATCHWORK DRESS PANEL

See Notes on p. 42 before continuing.

30 Lay out the labeled cotton print pieces (A–F) as shown in diagram A on p. 49.

31 Assemble Row 2 by placing the 2 A pieces right sides together, pinning and then sewing along one short side. Add the C piece in the same manner and then press all seam allowances up, toward the A pieces. Repeat entire step with each even numbered row, attaching the pieces as shown in diagram A.

32 Now, place Rows 1 and 2 right sides together, pinning and then sewing along one long side (**figure 9**). Repeat to attach the rows in pairs (3 and 4, 5 and 6, etc. . . .) until you have 8 attached pairs.

33 Repeat Step 32 to attach the pairs to each other in the order shown in the diagram, until you have one patchwork panel (it will now measure 32½" x 7½" [82.5 x 19 cm]). Press all seam allowances to one side.

34 With the patchwork panel laying wrong side up in front of you, fold one short (7 1/2" [19 cm]) edge over toward the wrong side by 1/2" (1.3 cm) and press, then fold over another 1/2" (1.3 cm) and press again. Be sure to set your sewing machine back to the default settings for a straight stitch (p. 155). Edgestitch (p. 154) along the inner folded edge (just shy of 1/2" [1.3 cm] from the edge). Repeat entire step with the other short edge. Repeat again to hem one long edge of the patchwork panel (this will be the bottom of the dress).

35 Adjust the stitch length on your machine to the longest stitch length for basting (p. 154). Baste across the top (unhemmed) long edge of the patchwork panel, 1/2" (1.3 cm) from the edge; do not backtack (p. 154) at either end; leave long thread tails. Repeat to make a second line of basting stitches 1/8" (3 mm) below the first.

36 One on side of the patchwork panel, tie together the bobbin threads only, on the wrong side of the panel. Then, pick up the bobbin threads from the other side and gather the fabric by gently sliding it along the threads, until it measures 10" (25.5 cm) wide. Make sure that the gathers are distributed evenly, then tie the thread tails to secure the gathers in place; set aside.

MAKE AND ATTACH THE WAISTBAND

37 Return the stitch length on your machine to the default setting (see your sewing machine manual for assistance). Take the linen waistband piece (10 1/2" x 3" [26.5 x 7.5 cm]) and fold over each edge, toward the wrong side, by 1/4" (6 mm) and press. Then, fold the waistband in half lengthwise, with wrong sides together, and press.

38 Place the gathered edge of the patchwork panel inside the waistband by about 1/2" (1.3 cm), so that the waistband encases the edge and just covers the top line of

Diagram B

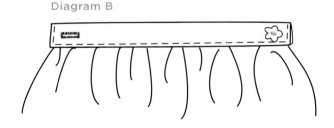

basting stitches. Pin in place, then hand-baste (p. 154) the waistband to the patchwork panel, about 1/8" (3 mm) from the bottom edge of the waistband. Remove the pins.

39 Edgestitch, through all layers, along both side edges and the bottom edge of the waistband, checking as you go that the bottom of the waistband is being caught in the stitches; begin stitching at the top of one side of the waistband, pivoting at the corner without lifting the needle to sew

Diagram A

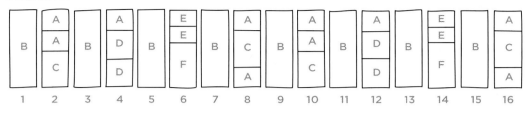

| 1 | 2 | 3 | 4 | 5 | 6 | 7 | 8 | 9 | 10 | 11 | 12 | 13 | 14 | 15 | 16 |

along the bottom edge, then pivoting again at the second corner to finish stitching up the side (see diagram B at left). Then, gently remove the basting stitches from the waistband and the patchwork panel, using a seam ripper.

FINISHING

40 Use a water-soluble fabric pen or tailor's chalk to draw a ³/₄" (2 cm) long horizontal "I" shape at one short edge of the waistband, ¹/₄" (6 mm) below the top edge and ¹/₄" (6 mm) over from the side (see diagram B; the bars at the top and bottom of the "I" shape should only be about ³/₁₆" [4 mm] long). This will be the guide for creating the buttonhole. Check the placement of the buttonhole by placing the patchwork dress around the lamb's body, just under her arms, bringing the two edges together at the center back. Adjust the placement of the buttonhole, if necessary, for a snug fit.

41 Switch to the buttonhole foot on your sewing machine and be sure to pull the slider forward. Set your machine to the buttonhole setting (since every machine is a little different, refer to your sewing machine manual for more information on the buttonhole settings and sewing buttonholes).

42 Place the waistband under the presser foot as you normally would (with the "I" shape perpendicular to you), the needle should be over the upper left side of your "I" shape. Sew the buttonhole.

43 Place straight pins at the top and bottom of the buttonhole opening to protect the bar tacking on either end. Carefully and slowly cut open the center of the buttonhole between the lines of stitching (you can use a seam ripper or X-Acto knife for this—the latter is my preference as it's sharper and makes cutting easier). Remove the pins.

44 Check the placement of the button by placing the patchwork dress around your lamb's body, just under her arms, bringing the two edges together at the center back as before. Overlap the buttonhole side of the waistband over the opposite side and mark the position of the button by marking through the center of the buttonhole with a fabric pen or tailor's chalk.

45 Handsew your button to the right side of the waistband on the mark you made in Step 44. Then, put the dress on the lamb, buttoning the waistband at the back.

finished size

20″ (51 cm) wide at waist (not including ties) x 19¼″ (49 cm) long. Apron is adjustable with ties (waistband plus ties: about 79½″ [2 m]).

materials

Linen *(shown: natural)*
  14½″ x 28½″ (37 x 72.5 cm) rectangle for skirt shell

  18″ x 35½″ (45.5 x 90 cm) rectangle for skirt lining

  20½″ x 5″ (52 x 11.5 cm) strip for waistband

  2 strips, each 30½″ x 4″ (77.5 x 10 cm) for ties

  6½″ x 6½″ (16.5 x 16.5 cm) square for pocket lining

Various cotton prints
(7 different prints shown)
  18 squares, each 4″ x 4″ (10 x 10 cm) for skirt border

  9 squares, each 2½″ x 2½″ (6.5 x 6.5 cm) for pocket

Fusible interfacing
  20″ x 4″ (51 x 10 cm) strip for waistband

patchwork bordered APRON

Sometimes I wish you could wear an apron all the time as part of your regular wardrobe. Of course, only if your apron is worthy of such adoration. This sweet linen apron is not only practical but eye-catching as well. With a wide patchwork border and a convenient pocket, this apron is sure to become a favorite accessory, perhaps even outside the kitchen.

Patchwork Bordered Apron

Note: All seam allowances are ¼" (6 mm) unless otherwise indicated.

ASSEMBLE PATCHWORK BORDERS

1 Lay out the cotton skirt border squares (4" x 4" [10 x 10 cm]) in a border arrangement as shown in the diagram at right, with 5 squares on each side (vertical rows) and 8 squares across the bottom (horizontal row), placing the prints in the desired order.

2 Once you are happy with the layout of the squares, begin stitching the squares in the vertical rows together by placing 2 of them right sides together, matching up all the edges. Stitch them together along one edge. Continue adding squares in this manner to create a vertical row of 5 squares (it will measure 4" x 18" [10 x 45.5 cm]). Press all seam allowances toward the bottom. Repeat entire step to sew the remaining vertical row together.

3 Repeat Step 2 to sew the horizontal row of 8 squares together (it will measure 4" x 28½" [10 x 72.5 cm]). Press all seam allowances open. You now have 3 patchwork borders.

ASSEMBLE SKIRT SHELL

4 With the linen skirt shell (14½" x 28½" [37 x 72.5 cm]) facing right side up, place the horizontal patchwork border (8 squares) on top, right side down, matching up the 28½" (72.5 cm) edges. Pin n place, then stitch together along the pinned

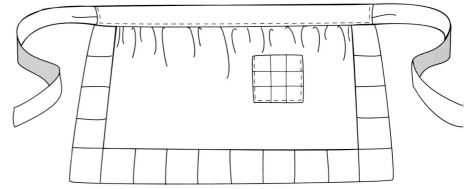

edge. Press the seam allowances toward the patchwork border.

5 Repeat Step 4 to attach 1 vertical patchwork border (5 squares) to each side of the skirt shell. The bordered skirt shell now measures 18" (45.5 cm) long x 35½" (90 cm) wide.

ASSEMBLE AND ATTACH POCKET

6 Arrange the 9 pocket squares (2½" x 2½" [6.5 x 6.5 cm]) into three rows of 3 (see the diagram above for assistance), placing colors as desired.

7 Repeat Step 2 to stitch together three vertical rows of 3 squares each. Press all seam allowances up.

8 Stitch the three vertical rows together to form a square that is 3 squares high x 3 squares across (it will measure 6½" x 6½" [16.5 x 16.5 cm]). Press the seam allowances to the left. You now have the completed patchwork pocket.

9 Place the patchwork pocket right sides together with the linen pocket lining piece.

Match up all the edges evenly and pin together around the perimeter.

10 Stitch the pocket pieces together around the perimeter, leaving a 2″ (5 cm) gap for turning. Clip the corners (p. 157).

11 Turn the pocket inside out and push out the corners (use the point turner if necessary). Turn in the seam allowances of the opening and handstitch closed with a slipstitch (p. 156). Press the pocket flat.

12 With the skirt shell facing right side up, pin on the pocket where you want it. Topstitch the pocket to the skirt shell, $1/8''$ (3 mm) from the edge around the sides and bottom, leaving the top open. Pivot at the corners as you stitch, without lifting the needle, for a continuous stitch line (see sewing a corner on p. 18).

ATTACH THE SKIRT LINING

13 Place the skirt shell right sides together with the linen skirt lining piece (18″ x 35½″ [45.5 x 90 cm]), lining up all the edges, and pin together around the perimeter.

14 Stitch the apron pieces together along the sides and bottom, leaving the top open (this will be closed later).

15 Clip the bottom corners and turn the apron inside out. Push out the corners (use the point turner if necessary) and press the apron flat.

CREATE THE GATHERS

16 Adjust the stitch length on your machine to the longest stitch length for basting. Leaving thread tails at each end, machine-baste across the top of the apron skirt, through both layers, about ½" (1.3 cm) from the edge (do not tie off).

17 Machine-baste again, ⅛" (3 mm) below the previous stitch line, again leaving thread tails at both ends (do not tie off).

18 Take the bobbin threads only (one from each row of basting) and tie them together with a double overhand knot (p. 156) on one side of the apron.

19 Pick up the bobbin threads from the untied side and gather the fabric by gently pulling the threads and bunching the fabric evenly along the threads until it measures about 20" (51 cm) wide.

20 Tie the threads with a double overhand knot to secure the gathers and then trim all thread tails.

21 Adjust your sewing machine back to the standard stitch length and set the apron aside.

ASSEMBLE THE WAISTBAND AND TIES

See the diagram on p. 52 for assistance with the following steps.

22 Take 1 of the linen ties (30½" x 4" [77.5 x 10 cm]) and fold it in half lengthwise, with right sides together. Pin the layers together, then sew along one short side and the long side, leaving the remaining short side open for turning. Clip the corners and turn the tie right side out. Push out the corners (use the point turner if necessary) and press flat. Repeat entire step with the second tie; set both aside.

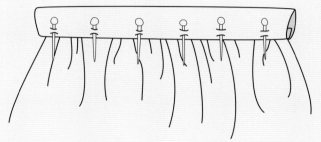

figure 1

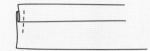

figure 2

23 Center the interfacing piece, fusible side down, on the wrong side of the linen waistband (20$\frac{1}{2}$" x 4$\frac{1}{2}$" [52 x 11.5 cm]) and fuse according to manufacturer's instructions.

24 Fold both short sides over, toward the wrong side, by $\frac{1}{4}$" (6 mm), and press. Fold the waistband in half lengthwise, with wrong sides together, and press.

25 Unfold the waistband (leaving the short sides folded under) and place it right sides together with the skirt, aligning the raw edge at the gathered waist with the raw edge at the top of the waistband; pin together securely, ensuring the gathers on the skirt remain evenly distributed.

26 Stitch together with a $\frac{1}{2}$" (1.3 cm) seam allowance. Trim the waistband seam allowance to $\frac{1}{4}$" (6 mm), then fold the waistband up and press along the seam line.

27 Fold the waistband raw edge over $\frac{1}{2}$" (1.3 cm) toward the wrong side and press. Then, fold the waistband along the existing crease down the center and place the folded-under edge against the lining of the skirt ($\frac{1}{2}$" [1.3 cm] down from the edge of the skirt) and pin in place; the edges of the waistband should be level with each other (**figure 1**) and the top line of basting should be covered by the waistband.

28 At the raw edge of each tie, make a $\frac{1}{4}$" (6 mm) pleat at the center and press (you will be inserting this end into the waistband, you may want to check the fit now to ensure that the ties will fit neatly into the side of the waistband). Stitch across the pleat to secure it in place, about $\frac{1}{4}$" (6 mm) from the raw edge (**figure 2**).

29 Slip the ends of the ties into the waistband by about $\frac{1}{2}$" (1.3 cm) and pin. Make sure all sides of the waistband are lined up.

30 Edgestitch (p. 154) the sides and bottom of the waistband. Remove the visible basting stitches (below the waistband) with a seam ripper. Now you're ready to cook something up in the kitchen!

finished size

Bag is about 15¼" (38.5 cm) long (not including handles) x 14½" (37 cm) wide x 2" (5 cm) deep (front to back) at the base. Bag is about 25" (63.5 cm) long with handles. Pocket is 4½" (11.5 cm) long x 6" (15 cm) wide.

materials

Linen *(shown: natural)*

35³/₄" x 15¹/₂" (90 x 39.5 cm) rectangle for bag

Various cotton prints *(2 different prints shown)*

12" x 7" (30.5 x 18 cm) rectangle for pocket

1 scrap, at least 3" x 3" (7.5 x 7.5 cm) for coverable button

2 strips, each 24" x 3" (61 x 7.5 cm) for handles

8¹/₂" x 2" (21.5 x 5 cm) strip for button loop

1 size 60 (1¹/₂" [3.8 cm]) coverable button

tools

Point turner (optional)

Loop turner (optional)

Blind-hem or edgestitch foot for sewing machine (optional)

fold—up eco BAG

Paper or plastic? How about linen instead? I love the thought of "going green" in any way possible, so why not do it with style? This eco-bag folds up nicely into its own pouch that will fit right into your purse, opening up into a roomy grocery bag when you hit the store or farmer's market With its convenient design and earth-friendly purpose, this irresistible tote will be a big hit!

Fold-Up Eco Bag

Notes: All seam allowances are $1/4''$ (6 mm) unless otherwise indicated.

+ When creating the pocket and the bag you will be following instructions for sewing French seams (p. 154), which involves turning the pieces several times and stitching the seams twice. If you've never used French seams, just trust me—follow the instructions and you'll have beautifully finished seams at the end.

CREATE THE POCKET

1 Take the pocket piece (12″ x 7″ [30.5 x 18 cm]) and fold over one long edge by $1/2''$ (1.3 cm), toward the wrong side, and press, then fold over another $1/2''$ (1.3 cm) and press.

2 Topstitch (p. 155) the fold about $3/8''$ (1 cm) from the edge.

3 With wrong sides together, fold the finished edge of the pocket over (folding the piece widthwise), placing it 1″ (2.5 cm) below the raw edge and matching up the side edges (**figure 1**); pin together at the sides.

4 Stitch together along the pinned edges. Trim the seam allowances to $1/8''$ (3 mm).

5 Turn the pocket inside out and push out the corners (use the point turner if necessary); press flat. Stitch the side seams again, $1/4''$ (6 mm) from the existing seam lines (**figure 2**). Turn the pocket right side out and push out the corners. This time press the entire pocket, especially along the seam allowances on the top 1″ (1.5 cm). Set the pocket aside.

ADD THE BUTTON AND BUTTON LOOP

6 Cover your coverable button with the cotton print scrap, according to manufacturer's instructions; set aside.

7 Fold over the long sides of the cotton print strip ($8 1/2''$ x 2″ [21.5 x 5 cm]) $1/2''$ (1.3 cm), toward the wrong side. Then, fold the strip in half lengthwise with wrong sides together, encasing the raw edges. Edgestitch (p. 154) along the folded-under edges to finish. You now have the button loop.

8 Fold the button loop in half, placing the ends next to each other to form a loop that will lie flat (**figure 3**).

9 Take your pocket and make a light mark, centered, $1 1/2''$ (3.8 cm) down from the raw edge on the back of the pocket.

10 Place the ends of the loop on the pocket at the mark made in Step 9, placing it so that the loop is facing toward the bottom edge of the pocket. Topstitch across the ends, about $1/8''$ (3 mm) from the edges of the loop, to secure it to the pocket (be careful not to stitch through the front of the pocket; **figure 4**). Fold the loop up toward the top edge of the pocket and stitch over the ends again, as before (**figure 5**).

11 Handsew your button to the front of the pocket, centered, $1 1/2''$ (3.8 cm) down from the finished edge (whipstitch [p. 157] in place to secure the button to the pocket). Set the pocket aside.

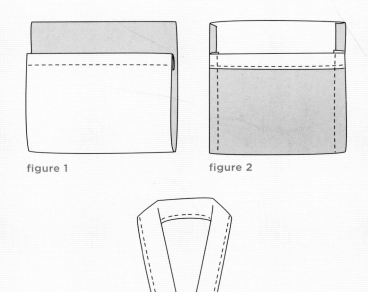

figure 1

figure 2

figure 3

figure 4

figure 5

CREATE THE HANDLES

12 Fold 1 of the handles (24″ x 3″ [61 x 7.5 cm]) in half lengthwise with right sides together. Stitch together along the long edge.

13 Turn the strip right side out (you can use a loop turner if desired). Press the handle flat so that the seam runs down the middle. Topstitch about ⅛″ (3 mm) from each long edge.

14 Repeat Steps 12 and 13 with the remaining handle; set the handles aside.

CREATE THE BAG

15 Take the linen bag piece (35¾″ x 15½″ [90 x 39.5 cm]) and fold under each short edge ½″ (1.3 cm) and press, then fold over another 1⅛″ (2.9 cm) and press.

See **figure 6** for assistance with Steps 16 and 17.

16 With the bag piece facing wrong side up, mark the placement for the handles along the folded edges by measuring in from each long side 3¾″ (9.5 cm). Use the marks as a guide for placing the ends of each handle, seam side down, about 1″ (2.5 cm) underneath the folds; pin in place.

17 Take the pocket and slip the raw edge underneath the folds between the ends of one of the handles, placing it 1″ (2.5 cm) underneath the fold so that the pocket opening is even with the folded edge; pin in place. The pocket should fit perfectly, touching the inside edges of the handle on each side.

18 Edgestitch (p. 154) along the bottom of each folded edge, stitching over the handles and the pocket.

19 Fold the handles up so that they are hanging past the hemmed edges, off the bag. Pin in place near the top of the folded edge. Edgestitch along the top of each folded edge, stitching over the handles (**figure 7**).

20 Fold the bag in half widthwise, with wrong sides together, lining up the side and top edges; pin together along the sides. Make sure the handles are out of the way and then stitch the side seams. Trim the seam allowances to 1/8" (3 mm). Clip the corners (p. 157), turn the bag inside out, and push out the corners (use the point turner if necessary); press flat.

21 Stitch the side seams again, 1/4" (6 mm) from the existing seam lines. Turn the bag right side out and push out the corners.

22 To square the corners, flatten one side seam of the bag on the table so that it lies directly down the center, forming a point at the corner. Using the acrylic ruler and fabric pen, measure about 1 1/2" (3.8 cm) down from the corner and mark, then draw a line across the corner (perpendicular to the side seam), through the mark (**figure 8**). Stitch along this line, then clip off the corner, about 1/4" (6 mm) above the stitch line (**figure 9**). Repeat entire step for the opposite corner.

23 Turn the bag inside out, flatten as before and stitch 1/4" (6 mm) from (and parallel to) the existing seam lines at each corner. Turn the bag right side out (last time, I promise) and push out the corners. You're done!

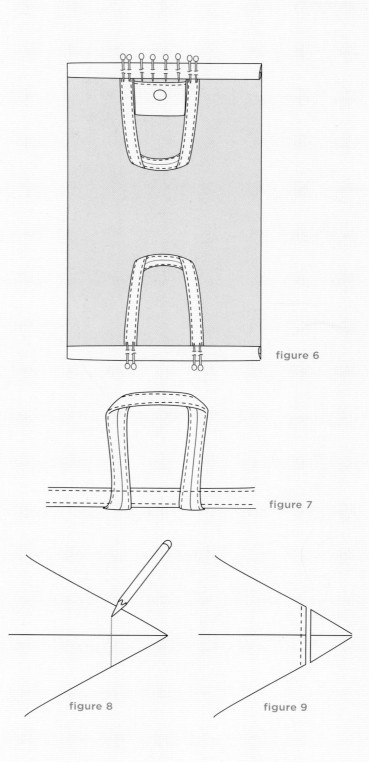

figure 6

figure 7

figure 8

figure 9

folding the bag

1 Flip the pocket over the top of the bag so that it is lying on the outside of the bag and then lay the bag down in front of you, with the pocket lying on top and the handles flipped down onto the bag (**figure 1**).

2 Fold over the sides of the bag so that the outer edges are flush with the sides of the pocket (**figure 2**).

3 Beginning at the bottom, fold the bag up three times (**figure 3**), then tuck the bag into the pocket. Pull the loop around the button and—voilà (**figure 4**)!

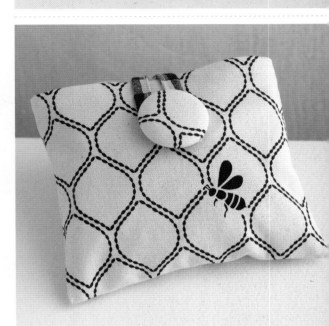

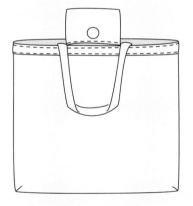

figure 1

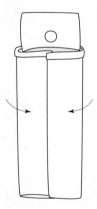

figure 2

figure 3

figure 4

lap QUILT

I was inspired to make this quilt after seeing a similar doll-size quilt made by one of my favorite bloggers at Soto Softies. The bursts of cheery color in between the linen patches are so wonderful, and I knew a large version would be just the thing. This quilt would be brilliant to have on hand for curling up with a good book and a cup of tea on a chilly afternoon. So this one's for you, Maritza!

Lap Quilt

Note: All seam allowances are ¼" (6 mm) unless otherwise indicated.

+ Seam allowances are already included in the cutting dimensions given for the quilt blocks.

+ Remember to wash and dry all fabric before cutting to prevent further shrinkage with subsequent washing.

CUT THE FABRIC

1 Cut the following pieces as directed.

FROM SOLID COTTON

Cut 2 rectangles, each 15½" x 30½" (39.5 x 77.5 cm) for quilt backing

Cut 2 squares, each 30½" x 30½" (77.5 x 77.5 cm) for quilt backing

FROM LINEN

Cut 2 rectangles, each 60½" (153.5 cm) long x 6½" (16.5 cm) wide for border

Cut 2 rectangles, each 48½" (123 cm) long x 6½" (16.5 cm) wide for border

2 Refer to the Quilt Top and Quilt Backing Stripe Cutting Charts to cut the cotton and linen pieces for the quilt, using a rotary cutter and self-healing mat (don't forget to square up your fabric before cutting; see p. 14). Set aside the quilt backing stripe pieces for now.

ASSEMBLE THE QUILT TOP

3 Lay out Rows 1–16, as shown in diagram A (on p. 66), for the quilt top. Begin sewing the pieces in each row together; place 2 of the pieces in Row 1 right sides together and match up along one short (3½" [9 cm]) edge and pin. Stitch along the pinned edge. Continue in this manner to attach all the pieces in each row. Press the seam allowances on each row in one direction, alternating every row (i.e., Row 1: press all seam allowances up, Row 2: press all seam allowances down, Row 3: press all seam allowances up, etc. . .).

4 Now, stitch the rows together in order; place Row 1 and Row 2 right sides together, aligning all edges, and pin along the long edge (see Patchwork Pinning on p. 16). Stitch together along the pinned edge. Continue in this manner until you have 1 patchwork panel measuring 48½" x 48½" (123 x 123 cm). Press all seam allowances in one direction.

5 Stitch the 2 vertical linen border pieces (48½" x 6½" [123 x 16.5 cm]) to the right and left sides of the assembled patchwork panel as shown in diagram B (p. 67). Press the seam allowances toward the linen. Repeat to attach the 2 horizontal linen border pieces (60½" x 6½" [153.5 x 16.5 cm]) to the top and bottom of the quilt.

6 Press the quilt top flat and set aside.

ASSEMBLE THE QUILT BACKING STRIPE

7 Lay out your quilt backing stripe pieces on a flat surface, according to diagram C (p. 68). You will be creating 4 blocks for the stripe, as shown, each measuring 15½" x 15½" (39.5 x 39.5 cm). Sew the pieces

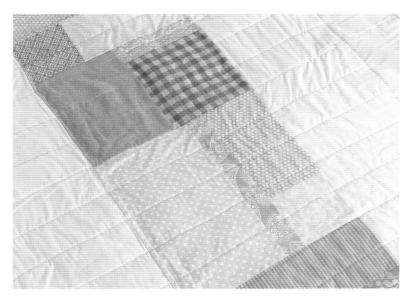

quilt top cutting chart

Cut the indicated number of pieces from each fabric (cotton prints A–O and linen) according to the measurements given at the top of each column. Use a water-soluble fabric pen or tailor's chalk to label each piece with the fabric letter and the number label given at the bottom of each column. For example, in the first row, the first 3 squares (3½" x 3½" [9 x 9 cm]) cut from the A fabric will be labeled A1 and the 2 rectangles (3½" x 9½" [9 x 24 cm]) will be labeled A3. Linen pieces will be marked with the number only.

FABRIC	3½" X 3½" (9 x 9 cm)	3½" X 6½" (9 x 16.5 cm)	3½" X 9½" (9 x 24 cm)
A	3	0	2
B	4	1	1
C	4	0	2
D	4	0	2
E	4	0	2
F	4	1	1
G	4	0	2
H	4	1	1
I	3	0	2
J	3	0	2
K	4	0	2
L	3	0	2
M	4	0	2
N	4	0	2
O	4	0	2
LINEN	53	2	19
NUMBER LABEL:	1	2	3

quilt backing stripe cutting chart

Cut each piece to the indicated measurements from the specified fabric (cotton prints a–o and linen). Use a water-soluble fabric pen or tailor's chalk to label each cotton print piece with the fabric letter (even if you decide to use the same fabric for several of the pieces, simply label each piece with the corresponding letter from the chart).

FABRIC	MEASUREMENTS
a	2" x 15" (5 x 38 cm)
b	5½" x 5½" (14 x 14 cm)
c	15½" x 10½" (4 x 26.5 cm)
d	15½" x 10½" (4 x 26.5 cm)
e	15½" x 10½" (4 x 26.5 cm)
f	7¾" x 8" (19.5 x 20.5 cm)
g	5½" x 5½" (14 x 14 cm)
h	8" x 11¼" (20.5 x 28.5 cm)
i	9" x 15½" (23 x 39.5 cm)
j	4½" x 15½" (12 x 39.5 cm)
k	5½" x 15½" (14 x 39.5 cm)
l	5½" x 15½" (14 x 39.5 cm)
m	5½" x 5½" (14 x 14 cm)
n	8" x 11¼" (20.5 x 28.5 cm)
o	3" x 7¾" (7.5 x 19.5 cm)
LINEN	8¼" x 10½" (21 x 26.5 cm)

1	2	3	4	5	6	7	8	9	10	11	12	13	14	15	16

Column 1: A3, 1, 1, I3, O1, 1, L3, N1, 1, 1

Column 2: B1, A1, 3, 1, I, O3, 1, 1, L1, N3, 1

Column 3: B2, C1, 1, 3, E1, O1, 1, 3, F1, N1, 2

Column 4: B1, C3, J1, 1, E3, 1, 1, A1, F3, 1, 1

Column 5: 1, D1, C1, 1, J3, 1, E1, A1, F1, M1, 3, 1

Column 6: D3, J1, 3, G1, 1, 1, A3, M3, 1

Column 7: K1, D1, 3, L1, 1, G3, 1, A1, M3, 1, H1

Column 8: K2, E1, 1, L3, D1, G1, 3, 1, M1, H2

Column 9: K1, E3, 1, L1, D3, 1, 1, N1, H1

Column 10: 1, 1, E1, 3, 1, D1, 3, 1, 3, N3, 1

Column 11: 3, H1, 1, 3, C1, 3, 3, O1, N1, 1

Column 12: F1, 1, H3, 1, C3, 1, B1, 1, O3, 1

Column 13: F2, 1, M1, H1, 3, K1, C1, 1, B3, 3, O1, 2

Column 14: F1, M3, G1, 1, K3, 1, 3, B1, J1, 1, I1, 1

Column 15: 1, 1, M1, G3, 1, K1, 3, J1, 1, I3, 1

Column 16: 3, 1, G1, 3, 1, 1, J3, I1, 1

together to create the blocks, then press all vertical seam allowances to the right and all horizontal seam allowances toward the bottom of the blocks.

8 Stitch the blocks together to create the stripe, sewing them together in order, end to end, forming one 15½" x 60½" (39.5 x 153.5 cm) stripe (see diagrams C and D on p. 68 for assistance). Press the seam allowances to the right. Set aside.

Refer to diagram D for assistance with Steps 9 and 10.

9 Place the two 15½" x 30½" (39.5 x 77.5 cm) quilt backing pieces right sides together, aligning all edges. Pin and then stitch together along one short (15½" [39.5 cm]) edge. Open up the unit and press the seam allowances open; you now have a 15½" x 60½" (39.5 x 152.5 cm) upper panel. Repeat entire step with the two 30½" x 30½" (77.5 x 77.5 cm) quilt backing pieces, stitching along one edge to create a 60½" x 30½" (153.5 x 77.5 cm) lower panel.

10 Finally, place the upper panel and the patchwork stripe right sides together, pinning and then stitching along the top 60½" (153.5 cm) edge. Open up the newly created unit and press the seam allowances

Diagram B

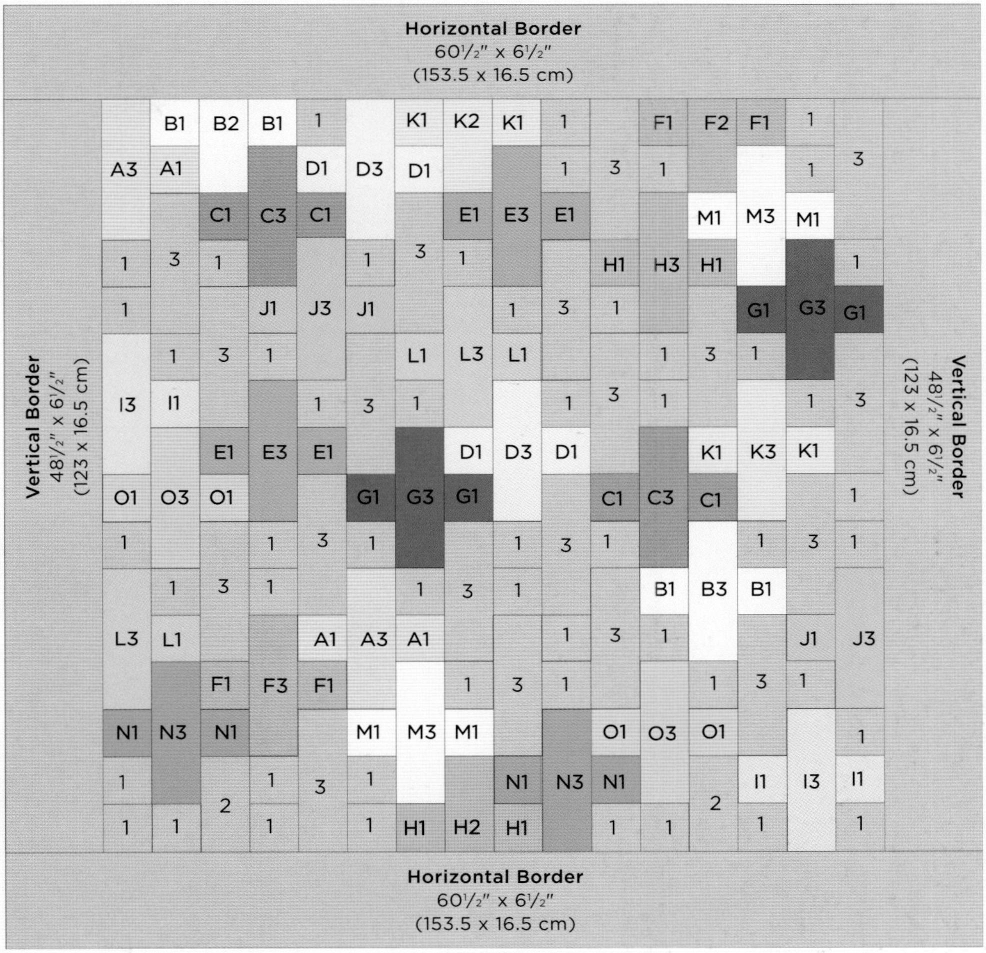

Horizontal Border
60½" x 6½"
(153.5 x 16.5 cm)

Vertical Border
48½" x 6½"
(123 x 16.5 cm)

Vertical Border
48½" x 6½"
(123 x 16.5 cm)

	B1	B2	B1	1		K1	K2	K1	1		F1	F2	F1	1	
A3	A1			D1	D3	D1			1	3	1			1	3
		C1	C3	C1			E1	E3	E1			M1	M3	M1	
1	3	1			1	3	1			H1	H3	H1			1
1			J1	J3	J1			1	3	1			G1	G3	G1
	1	3	1			L1	L3	L1			1	3	1		
I3	I1			1	3	1			1	3	1			1	3
		E1	E3	E1			D1	D3	D1			K1	K3	K1	
O1	O3	O1			G1	G3	G1			C1	C3	C1			1
1			1	3	1			1	3	1			1	3	1
	1	3	1			1	3	1		B1	B3	B1			
L3	L1			A1	A3	A1			1	3	1			J1	J3
		F1	F3	F1			1	3	1			1	3	1	
N1	N3	N1			M1	M3	M1			O1	O3	O1			1
1			1	3	1			N1	N3	N1			I1	I3	I1
1	1		2	1		1	H1	H2	H1		1	1	2	1	1

Horizontal Border
60½" x 6½"
(153.5 x 16.5 cm)

open. Repeat entire step to attach the lower panel to the free side of the stripe. You now have the completed 60½" x 60½" (153.5 x 153.5 cm) quilt backing.

FINISHING

To finish the quilt as shown here, without a binding, continue with the following steps. To finish the quilt with a bound edge, see the sidebar on p. 69.

11 Lay the batting down on a clean hard floor or other large surface. Smooth it out until it's nice and flat and then tape down the edges with masking tape to hold it temporarily in place. Center the quilt backing on top (right side up), and then place the quilt top on top of the backing (right side down; the batting will hang past the edges of the quilt backing and top). Pin all layers together, around the edges.

Diagram C

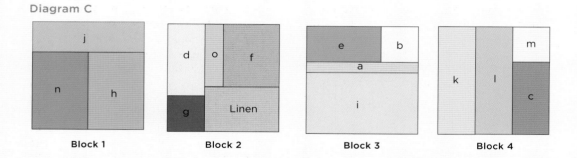

Block 1   Block 2   Block 3   Block 4

Diagram D

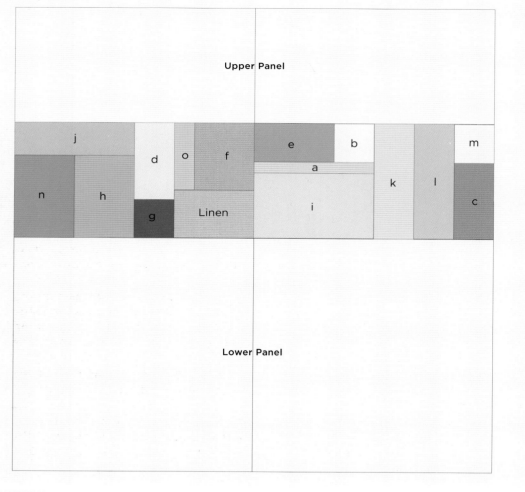

12 Trim the excess batting, then stitch the layers together, around the entire edge, leaving an opening on one edge large enough for turning. Clip the corners (p. 157) and then turn the quilt right side out. Push out the corners (use a point turner if necessary). Turn in the seam allowances at the opening by $1/4$" (6 mm) and press. Then handstitch the opening closed with a slip stitch (p. 156).

13 Hand-baste or pin the layers of the quilt together; with handsewing needle and thread or bent-arm safety pins, start at the center and work your way out, hand-basting or pinning in vertical rows (from the top to bottom edge of the patchwork panel), no more than 6" (15 cm) apart. If you are using safety pins, be sure that there is at least one pin every 6" (15 cm) and be careful while sewing, removing any pins that may get in the way of your stitching.

14 Switch to the walking foot on your machine, then machine quilt as follows: Topstitch around the perimeter of the quilt, $1/4$" (6 mm) from the edge. Then, stitch in the ditch (p. 155) on the seams between each row of the patchwork panel, stopping at the borders (do not stitch onto the border). Finish by stitching in the ditch on the seams attaching the borders to the patchwork panel. Remove any remaining pins or the basting stitches.

finishing with a bound edge

1 To finish your quilt with a bound edge, buy $1/2$" (1.3 cm) double-fold binding (or the desired size) or make your own, according to the instructions under Patchwork Binding on p. 20 (this will create $1/2$" [1.3 cm] wide finished binding; $1/2$ yd [46 cm] of 45" [114.5 cm] wide fabric is sufficient). You can make patchwork binding as directed or simply a solid binding by using the same fabric for all strips. Set aside the finished binding.

To create a different binding width, multiply the desired finished width by 4 to obtain the necessary length for the strips.

2 Lay the quilt backing on a clean hard floor or other large surface (right side down). Smooth it out until it's nice and flat and then tape down the edges with masking tape to hold it temporarily in place. Center the batting on top and then place the quilt top on top of the backing (right side up), aligning the edges of the quilt top with the edges of the quilt backing. Trim the excess batting.

3 Follow the instructions in Step 13 to baste the layers together, basting them all the way from the outer edges of the quilt border. Then, follow the instructions in Step 14 to machine quilt.

4 Follow the instructions under Squaring up Quilts on p. 157, then follow the instructions under Attach Binding with Mitered Corners on p. 21 to bind the edges of the quilt with the binding. This method will change the finished size of the quilt to $60^{1}/_{2}$" x $60^{1}/_{2}$" (153.5 x 163.5 cm).

4³/₄" (12 cm) diameter. Each pincushion "petal" is about 1¹/₂" (3.8 cm), measured across the top.

materials

Linen *(shown: natural)*
  1 scrap, at least 4" x 4" (10 x 10 cm)

Various cotton prints *(5 different prints shown)*
  5 scraps, each at least 4" x 4" (10 x 10 cm)

Fiberfill

1 seven-well porcelain flower palette (4³/₄" [12 cm] diameter)

Strong thread

Paper or card stock for template

tools

Hot glue gun and glue sticks

Blossom Pincushion template (p. 151)

Copy machine (optional)

blossom PINCUSHION

This pretty pincushion is one of my favorite sewing room accessories. Having my pincushion constantly at my fingertips is essential while I sew, so I love that the porcelain dish base on this pincushion helps it to stay put and not roll about when I'm trying to use it. The well in the center is also perfect for holding buttons or other little notions that you may need for a project. And gosh—it's just so cute, don't you think?

Blossom Pincushion

1 Trace or copy the Blossom Pincushion template onto paper or card stock (card stock makes a sturdier template) and cut out.

2 Using the Blossom Pincushion template, trace one circle onto the wrong side of each of the cotton print scraps and the linen scrap with a water-soluble fabric pen or tailor's chalk; now would be a good time to plug in your glue gun to allow it to heat up for use in Step 6.

MAKE PINCUSHION POUFS

3 Take 1 of the fabric circles and with the needle and thread, hand-baste (p. 154) evenly around the edge of the pincushion top (about 1/4" [6 mm] from the edge) leaving a tail at each end; do not tie off.

4 Place some fiberfill in the center of the basted circle and gently pull your threads to begin gathering the pouf (**figure 1**).

5 Keep adding fiberfill until the pouf is quite firm. Place your pouf in one of the wells to be sure that it fits. You may have to add or remove some of the fiberfill. Pull the threads to close the pouf completely, then securely knot and trim your thread. Set aside.

6 Repeat Steps 3–5 to form poufs from the 5 remaining fabric circles.

ATTACH POUFS TO THE PALETTE

7 Use your hot glue gun to put some glue into the bottom of one of the outer wells of the flower palette. Place a pouf immediately

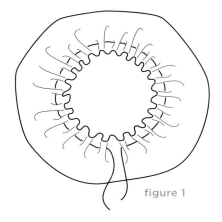

figure 1

into the well, on top of the glue, gathered side down. Press down firmly for a few seconds to allow the glue to form a strong bond. Repeat entire step five more times to add a pouf to each of the outer wells of the flower palette. Leave the center well free for holding buttons, beads, or other bits and pieces.

materials

Linen *(shown: natural)*

PLACEMAT:

12½" x 18½" (31.5 x 47 cm)
rectangle for back

12½" x 10" (31.5 x 25.5 cm)
square for front middle panel

2 strips, each 12½" x 2" (31.5 x
5 cm) for front side panels

3 strips, each 6½" x 1½" (16.5 x
3.8 cm) for stamped panels

NAPKIN:

16" x 16" (40.5 x 40.5 cm)
square

Various cotton prints *(6 different prints shown)*

PLACEMAT:

6 strips, each 3½" x 1½"
(9 x 3.8 cm)

NAPKIN:

1" x 37" (2.5 x 94 cm) strip
for ties

tools

Letter stamp set and black ink
pad (recommended: Versa-
Craft)

Blind hem or edgestitch foot
for sewing machine (optional)

placemat & napkin SET

As crazy as it sounds, sometimes I just plain forget the proper order for the utensils when setting the dinner table. I thought to myself, why not stamp the placemats as a clever reminder? No one need ever know that it is more than a charming decoration. Finish off each place setting with a lovely linen napkin, folded and tied neatly with a coordinating cotton tie.

Placemat

Notes: All seam allowances are $1/4''$ (6 mm) unless otherwise indicated.

+ It is important to choose an ink pad that is specifically for stamping on fabric, like Versa Craft, which dries quickly and becomes permanent when ironed.

STAMP THE LINEN

1 First, do a few practice stamps on scrap fabric with the letter stamps and ink pad—this will give you a chance to play around with the letter spacing. On each of the panels for stamping ($6^{1}/_{2}''$ x $1^{1}/_{2}''$ [16.5 x 3.8 cm]), stamp the name of a utensil: Knife, Fork, and Spoon, with the letters running in a vertical line (see the diagram at right).

ASSEMBLE THE PLACEMAT TOP

See the diagram at right for assistance with the following steps.

2 Place 1 of the cotton strips ($3^{1}/_{2}''$ x $1^{1}/_{2}''$ [9 x 3.8 cm]) right sides together with 1 of the stamped panels (created in Step 1), matching them up along a short ($1^{1}/_{2}''$ [3.8 cm]) edge; stitch together. Repeat entire step to attach another cotton strip to the opposite end of the stamped panel. You now have a long panel with the lettering in the middle and a cotton print on each end. Repeat entire step twice more with the remaining stamped panels and cotton strips. Press all seam allowances toward the cotton prints.

3 With right sides together, place the "Spoon" panel on top of the "Knife" panel and stitch together along the right-hand

TIP

You can use a $1/4''$ (6 mm) bias tape maker to fold the ties, if desired. This handy little device, available at many fabric stores, makes folding up bias tape a quick job! Simply follow manufacturer's instructions to run the fabric through the bias tape maker and press.

long edge (so that the "Spoon" panel ends up on the right-hand side). Press the seam allowances open; set aside.

4 Place the "Knife/Spoon" panel right sides together with 1 of the front side panels ($12^{1}/_{2}''$ x 2'' [31.5 x 5 cm]), matching up the edges. Stitch together along the right-hand long edge; press the seam allowances toward the "Knife/Spoon" panel. Repeat entire step to attach the remaining front side panel to the "Fork" panel, stitching together along the left-hand long edge.

5 Place the "Knife/Spoon" panel and front middle panel right sides together, matching up the right-hand edges. Stitch together along the right-hand edge and then press the seam allowances toward the "Knife/Spoon" panel. Repeat entire step to attach the "Fork" panel to the left-hand edge of the front middle panel. You now have the completed placemat top.

FINISH THE PLACEMAT

6 Place the completed placemat top and the linen back piece right sides together. Stitch together around the edge, leaving at least a 4'' (10 cm) gap for turning.

7 Clip the corners (p. 157) and turn the placemat right side out. Turn in the seam allowances at the gap by $1/4''$ (6 mm) and

Diagram

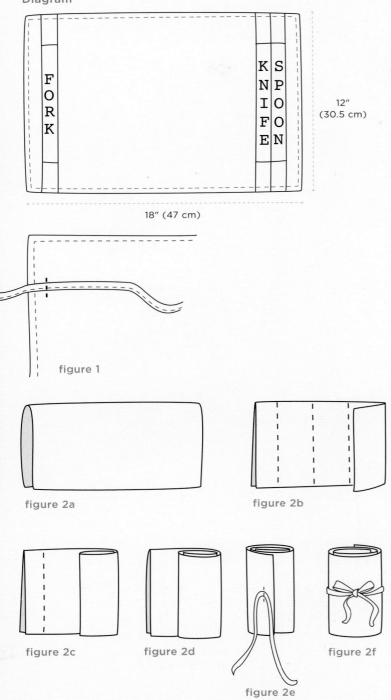

12" (30.5 cm)

18" (47 cm)

FORK

KNIFE SPOON

figure 1

figure 2a

figure 2b

figure 2c

figure 2d

figure 2e

figure 2f

press, then edgestitch (p. 154) around the perimeter of the placemat.

Napkin

8 Follow the instructions under Creating Hems with Mitered Corners on p. 19 to hem the napkin edges.

9 Topstitch (p. 155) $3/8$" (1 cm) from the edge around the perimeter of the napkin, pivoting at the corners with the needle still down, for a continuous stitch line (see Sewing a Corner on p. 18 for assistance).

CREATE THE TIES

10 Take the 1" x 37" (2.5 x 94 cm) cotton strip and fold the short raw edges over $1/2$" (1.3 cm), toward the wrong side; press. Fold the long raw edges over $1/4$" (6 mm), toward the wrong side (the raw edges will meet in the middle), and press.

11 Fold the strip in half lengthwise with wrong sides together, enclosing the raw edges, and press. Edgestitch along the matched edges.

12 Place your napkin in front of you, right side up. Fold the tie in half widthwise to find the center and finger press. Place the center of the tie $3 3/4$" (9.5 cm) from the top edge and 1" (2.5 cm) in from the left edge of the napkin. Topstitch the tie to the napkin, backtacking (p. 154) once or twice over the tie to secure (**figure 1**).

13 Place the napkin in front of you, wrong side up, so that the tie is lying on the left-hand side. Fold the napkin as shown in **figure 2**, first folding in half widthwise, then folding over about 4" (10 cm) three times, and folding the remaining left edge over the napkin (the last flap will be about 2" [5 cm] wide; **figure 2e**). Finally, flip the napkin over, bringing the ties around the sides and tie them in a pretty bow (**figure 2f**).

coaster SET

These coasters are like pretty little mini quilts, with the added bonus of providing protection for your furniture. These little beauties can make teatime even more enjoyable. They're quick and easy to create and they make a thoughtful and useful gift. Make them in colors to match the *Zigzag Table Runner* (p. 144) and the *Placemat and Napkin Set* (p. 74) and watch your dining room come alive!

Coaster Set

Note: All seam allowances are ¼" (6 mm) unless otherwise indicated.

1 Cut 4 squares, each 4½" x 4½" (11.5 x 11.5 cm) and one 6½" x 6½" (16.5 x 16.5 cm) from the batting; set aside (**figure 1**).

MAKING THE COASTER TOPS

2 Arrange your coaster top strips (1½" x 10" (3.8 x 25.5 cm) into 2 groups of 4. Begin stitching the strips from 1 group together by placing 2 of the strips right sides together and aligning all edges. Pin the strips together along one long edge, then sew along the pinned edge. Add the remaining 2 strips from the group in the same manner so that you have a 4-strip panel measuring 4½" (11.5 cm) wide x 10" (25.5 cm) long. Press all seam allowances in one direction. Repeat entire step to create another 4-strip panel with the second group of strips.

3 With your acrylic ruler and rotary cutter, cut each panel into 4 strips across the width so that each measures 2½" x 4½" (6.5 x 11.5 cm), using the edge of the ruler as a guide to make straight cuts. You should have a total of 8 strips.

4 Now pair 1 strip from the first group with 1 strip from the second group. Place them right sides together, making sure that the seam allowances are facing opposite directions and the seams and edges are all aligned (see Patchwork Pinning on p. 16. Pin them together along one 4½" (11.5 cm) edge. Sew along the pinned edge. You now have 1 coaster top. Repeat entire step to create 3 more coaster tops with the remaining strips.

ASSEMBLE THE COASTERS

5 Layer 1 of each of the following pieces in this order: batting square, coaster top (right side up), waffle fabric square (right

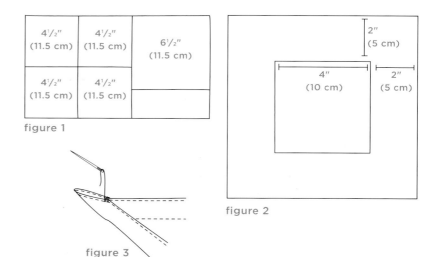

figure 1

figure 2

figure 3

side down). Line up all the edges and pin the layers together.

6 Stitch the layers together around the perimeter, leaving at least a 2" (5 cm) opening along one side for turning.

7 Clip the corners (p. 157) and then turn the coaster inside out. Push out the corners (use a point turner if necessary).

8 Tuck in the seam allowances at the opening by ¼" (6 mm) and press. Handsew the opening closed, using a slip stitch (p. 156).

9 Repeat Steps 4–8 to create 3 more coasters.

10 If you choose to quilt the coasters, you can do that now. Quilt the coasters using your preferred method and pattern. To machine quilt the coasters as shown here, follow the instructions in the Quilt Design sidebar at right and use the walking foot if desired. Alternatively, you could use a running stitch (p. 157) to quilt the coasters by hand, creating a grid, swirls, or any other pattern you like!

CREATE THE COASTER TRAY

11 Layer the following pieces in this order: 6½" x 6½" (16.5 x 16.5 cm) square of bat-

quilt design

Find the center of each print rectangle that makes up the coaster top and mark each at the top edge with a water-soluble fabric marker or tailor's chalk. Then, draw 4 zigzag lines across the coaster, 1 for each strip of 2 rectangles that makes up the coaster top. Using the water-soluble fabric marker or tailor's chalk and an acrylic ruler, draw a triangle shape on each rectangle of the coaster top by drawing diagonal lines from the bottom outside edge to the center mark, then down to the bottom of the rectangle at the seam line, back up to the next center mark, then down to the bottom outside edge of the rectangle, as shown in the diagram.

Using the drawn lines as a guide, quilt the coaster with a straight stitch (p. 155). Finish by edgestitching (p. 154) around the perimeter of the coaster. Remove any remaining pen marks with water or according to manufacturer's instructions.

Diagram

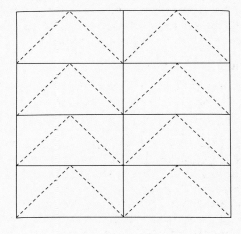

ting, cotton print tray lining (right side up), linen tray shell (right side down). Line up all the edges and pin the layers together.

12 Repeat Steps 6–8 with the pinned layers.

13 Press the tray flat, then edgestitch (p. 154) around the perimeter.

14 Place the tray in front of you, lining side up, and use an acrylic ruler and a hera marker to mark a 4" (10 cm) square, centered, in the middle of the tray. To find the corners of your inner square, measure over 2" (5 cm) from one corner (along one edge), then measure down 2" (5 cm) from this point and mark. Repeat at each corner. Connect the marks with straight lines (parallel to the edge), being sure to keep each line 2" (5 cm) from the edge. Alternatively, you can simply use the grid on your clear acrylic ruler to create the square by lining up one of the grid lines along each edge to find the point 2" (5 cm) in from each edge and then marking the first 4" (10 cm) line. Repeat on each side to create the 4" (10 cm) square (**figure 2**).

15 Topstitch (p. 155) along the marked lines, through all layers.

16 With the tray still lining side up, pinch the edges together, 1/2" (1.3 cm) below one corner, then secure the edges together by using a needle and one strand of embroidery floss to whipstitch (p. 157) in place two or three times (**figure 3**). Secure with a knot hidden in the fold and trim the thread. Repeat entire step at the three remaining corners.

Place your coasters in the tray and Enjoy!

materials

For 1 magnet

Linen *(shown: natural)*
  2½" x 4½" (6.5 x 11.5 cm)
  rectangle for pincushion top

Various cotton prints *(shown: 2 different prints)*
  2½" x 4½" (6.5 x 11.5 cm)
  rectangle for pincushion top

  1 scrap, at least 2¼" x 2¼"
  (5.5 x 5.5 cm) scrap for magnet
  cover

Lace trim or rickrack
(optional)
  3½" (9 cm)

Small amount of fiberfill for
stuffing

Thin chipboard (at least 1¼" x
1¼" [3.2 x 3.2 cm]) for pincushion bottom

Permanent fabric adhesive
(recommended: Fabri-Tac)

¾" (2 cm) magnet disc (see
Note on p. 84)

Strong thread

Paper or card stock for
templates

tools

Mini Pincushion templates
(p. 151)

Hot glue gun and glue sticks

Why would you need pincushons in your kitchen? Why not?
These mini versions are perfect for the kitchen or anywhere else
you have a magnetic surface. Keep safety pins or a threaded
needle handy for those moments when a favorite outfit needs a
quick fix before you head out the door.

Mini Pincushion Magnet

Note: Make sure the magnet disc is strong enough to hold the pincushion in place. To test it, try pinning the chipboard and some fabric to a magnetic surface with the magnet. The magnetic bond should be strong and not slip easily. You may want to consider a heavy-duty neodymium magnet such as Super Magnet. But beware, these magnets are super strong, so you may want to choose a smaller disc if using one of these.

1 Trace the Mini Pincushion templates onto paper or card stock (card stock will make a sturdier template) and cut out. Use a water-soluble fabric marking pen or tailor's chalk to trace the templates onto the wrong side of the fabrics indicated below and complete as directed (set aside Pincushion Top template for use in Step 6):

> Cut 1 magnet cover from cotton print scrap
>
> Cut 1 pincushion bottom from chipboard

CREATE THE PINCUSHION BOTTOM

2 Take the magnet cover piece and cut small slits into the edge at intervals, each about $1/4''$ (6 mm) apart (and no more than $3/16''$ [5 mm] long), around the circle (**figure 1**).

3 Place the pincushion bottom piece (chipboard) in front of you and carefully apply Fabri-Tac around the edge. Be careful not to let too much glue accumulate in one place.

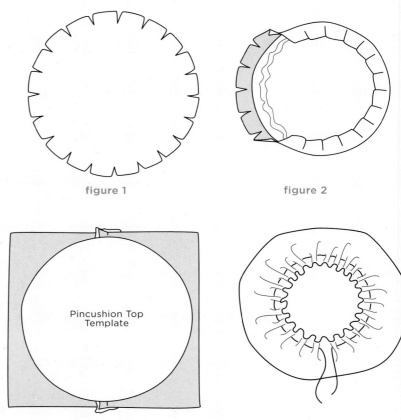

figure 1

figure 2

Pincushion Top Template

figure 3

figure 4

4 Place the pincushion bottom glue side up, centered, on the wrong side of the magnet cover. Fold the edges of the magnet cover over the edges of the pincushion bottom, pressing them into the glue (**figure 2**). Press with your finger to smooth the edges and set aside to dry. Now would be a good time to heat up your hot glue gun.

CREATE THE PINCUSHION TOP

5 Lay the linen rectangle right side up in front of you. If you are using the optional trim, place it on the linen, aligning the trim with one long (4½" [11.5 cm]) raw edge. Place the cotton rectangle on top, right side down, matching up all edges. Stitch through all layers along the edge with the trim, using a ¼" (6 mm) seam allowance (if you aren't using the trim, simply stitch through the two layers along one long edge). Press the seam allowances toward the linen.

6 Place the pincushion top template, centered, on the wrong side of the linen/cotton piece (assembled in Step 5; **figure 3**). Trace around it with a fabric pencil and cut out the circle. You now have the pincushion top.

7 With the needle and thread, hand-baste (p. 154) evenly around the edge of the pincushion top, leaving a tail at each end; do not tie off.

8 Pull the thread tails to carefully gather up the pincushion top a little (**figure 4**). Stuff with enough of the fiberfill for the top to be firm. Place the magnet, centered, on top of the fiberfill. Pull the threads to tightly close the pincushion top around the magnet and fiberfill. Secure the threads with a double overhand knot (p. 156) and clip the threads.

FINISHING

9 Take your hot glue gun and place some glue in the center of the wrong side of the pincushion bottom. Use enough glue for a secure bond, but be careful not to use too much as it could ooze out the sides.

10 Now quickly press the top and bottom together, with the bottom centered at the underside of the pincushion top (covering the gathering thread). Hold for a moment to make a secure bond, then set aside to dry completely.

16¹/₂" x 12¹/₂" (42 x 31.5 cm)

materials

Linen *(shown: natural)*
　17" x 13" (43 x 33 cm) rectangle
　for pillow front

　2 rectangles, each 10" x 13"
　(25.5 x 33 cm) for pillow back

Various cotton prints *(8 different prints shown)*
　8 different print strips, each
　1¹/₂" x 24" (3.8 x 61 cm) for strap

　3³/₄" x 3³/₄" (9.5 x 9.5 cm)
　square for large square

　2¹/₂" x 2¹/₂" (6.5 x 6.5 cm)
　square for small square

　1 scrap, at least 5" x 5"
　(12.5 x 12.5 cm) for large yo-yo

　1 scrap, at least 3¹/₂" x 3¹/₂"
　(9 x 9 cm) for small yo-yo

　2 scraps, each at least 1¹/₂" x
　1¹/₂" (3.8 x 3.8 cm) for covering
　buttons

Light interfacing
　3³/₄" x 3³/₄" (9.5 x 9.5 cm)
　square for large square

　2¹/₂" x 2¹/₂" (6.5 x 6.5 cm)
　square for small square

2 size 30 (³/₄" [2 cm]) coverable
buttons with kit

12" x 16" (30.5 x 40.5 cm)
pillow form

Silk thread for hand appliqué
(optional)

Paper or card stock for
templates

tools

X-Acto knife or box cutter
(optional)

Yo-yo templates (p. 151)

Point turner (optional)

Blind hem or edgestitch foot
for sewing machine (optional)

Blunt pencil or knitting needle

appliquéd PILLOW

This simple linen pillow has clean lines with a colorful patch-work tie and appliqué detail to add just the right accents. Use it as a throw pillow for your favorite chair or to brighten up the bed in your guest room. This pillow would be equally as lovely made up in a fabric to match your décor, with or without the appliqué embellishments.

Appliquéd Pillow

Note: All seam allowances are 1/4" (6 mm) unless otherwise indicated.

1 Trace the Large and Small Yo-yo templates onto paper or card stock (card stock will make a sturdier template) and cut out. Using a water-soluble fabric pen or tailor's chalk, trace one Large Yo-yo onto the wrong side of the larger cotton print scrap and cut out; repeat with the Small Yo-yo template and the smaller cotton print scrap; set both yo-yos aside.

PREPARE THE SQUARES

2 Lay the large square, right side down, on top of the large square interfacing (3 3/4" x 3 3/4" [9.5 x 9.5 cm]), matching up all the edges; pin together.

3 Stitch all the way around the perimeter of the square. With an X-Acto knife or scissors, gently cut a slit in the center of the interfacing only for turning the square (**figure 1**). Be careful not to cut into your cotton fabric.

4 Clip the corners (p. 157) and turn the square inside out, being careful not to rip the interfacing. Poke the corners out gently with the end of a blunt pencil or a knitting needle.

5 Repeat Steps 2–4 with the small square, then set both squares aside.

MAKE THE YO-YOS

6 If this is the first yo-yo you have made, it might be easier for you to start with the large yo-yo first. Thread the handsewing needle with a strand of thread and knot both ends together (p. 17) so that the thread will be doubled for use in Step 8.

7 Fold over the edges of the large yo-yo piece (cut in Step 1) about 1/4" (6 mm), toward the wrong side and finger press (p. 154).

8 Handstitch around the edge using a running stitch and leaving a thread tail. Stitch close to the edge, making small, even stitches (you'll probably have to refold the edge along the crease as you stitch). Work your way around the entire circle until you're back where you started. Do not tie off.

9 Once you've finished stitching, pull the threads to make the gathers of your yo-yo (**figure 2**), continuing to gather the edges until they are a tight circle. Spread the gathers evenly and make an overhand knot (p. 156) to secure the tails, then trim the threads. Flatten out the yo-yo.

10 Repeat Steps 6–9 to create the small yo-yo; set both aside.

ATTACH THE SQUARES

11 Place the linen pillow front (17" x 13" [43 x 33 cm]) flat in front of you, right side up. Place the large square near the bottom left corner, 3 1/4" (8.5 cm) up from the bottom edge and 2 1/4" (5.5 cm) over from the left edge. Pin in place.

12 Topstitch (p. 155) around the perimeter of the square, about 1/8" (3 mm) from the edge; pivot at the corners without lifting the needle for a continuous stitch line.

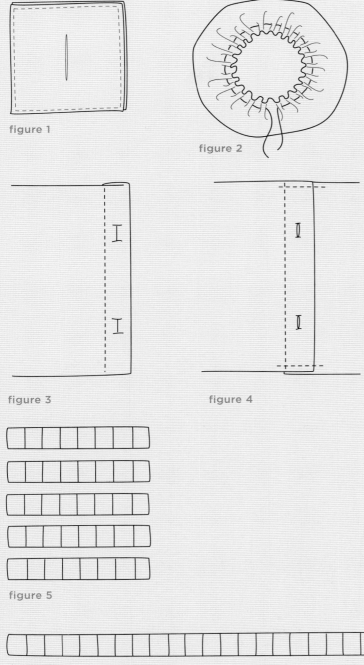

figure 1

figure 2

figure 3

figure 4

figure 5

figure 6

13 Center the small square on top of the right edge of the large square, placed so that about half is lying on top of the large square (see photo above). Topstitch around the perimeter of the square, about 1/8" (3 mm) from the edge; pivot at the corners without lifting the needle for a continuous stitch line.

HAND APPLIQUÉ THE YO-YOS

14 Pin the yo-yos in place over the squares (see photo above).

15 Thread your handsewing needle with one strand of silk thread, long enough to work the circumference of the yo-yo. You can use regular sewing thread for this if desired, but I prefer to use silk thread for appliqué because the stitches seem to almost disappear with the finer thread.

16 Handsew the yo-yo in place, around the edge, using a blindstitch (p. 156).

17 Continue stitching as in Step 16, making tiny stitches and working your way around the yo-yo. Once completed, push the needle back through to the wrong side of the pillow front and tie securely with an overhand knot (p. 156) on the wrong side.

18 Repeat Steps 15–17 with the remaining yo-yo.

CREATE THE BACK PANELS

19 On 1 linen back panel (10" x 13" [25.5 x 33 cm]), fold one of the short edges over ¼" (6 mm), toward the wrong side, and press, then fold it over again ¾' (2 cm) and press. Topstitch about ⅝" (1.5 cm) from the edge. Repeat entire step with the remaining back panel.

CREATE THE BUTTONHOLES

I suggest doing some practice buttonholes on a linen scrap before completing the following steps.

20 With 1 back panel facing right side up, use a pencil to mark a ⅞" (2.2 cm) long "I" shape on the panel, 4" (10 cm) down from the top edge and halfway between the folded edge and the stitch line (the bars at the top and bottom of the "I" shape should only be about 3/16" [4 mm] long). Repeat to draw a second "I" shape 4" (10 cm) up from the bottom edge (**figure 3**).

21 Switch to the buttonhole foot on your sewing machine and be sure to pull the slider forward. Set your machine to the buttonhole setting (since every machine is a little different, refer to your sewing machine manual for more information on the buttonhole settings and sewing buttonholes).

22 Place the back panel under the presser foot as you normally would (with the "I" shape perpendicular to you), the needle should be over the upper left side of your

"I" shape. Sew the buttonhole. Repeat to sew the second buttonhole.

23 Place straight pins at the top and bottom of the buttonhole opening to protect the bar tacking on either end. Carefully and slowly cut open the center of the buttonhole between the lines of stitching (you can use a seam ripper or X-Acto knife for this—the latter is my preference as it's sharper and makes cutting easier). Remove the pins.

ASSEMBLE THE PILLOW

24 Place the back panel pieces in front of you right side up. Overlap the hemmed edges by 1" (2.5 cm) with the buttonholes on top; make sure the top and bottom edges are aligned and then pin together. You now have a piece measuring 13" x 17" (33 x 43 cm). Stitch across the overlap about ⅛" (3 mm) from the top and bottom edges to hold the panels together (**figure 4**); remove the pins (you may want to leave a pin at the center to help hold the panels together).

25 With the back panels facing right side up, place the pillow front, right side down, on top and match up all edges. Pin together around the perimeter.

26 Stitch all the way around the perimeter of the pillow. Clip the corners (p. 157) and then turn the pillow right side out through the back panel opening (reach through and remove the pin at the center before turning). Push out the corners (use the point turner if necessary). You now have the completed pillowcase.

MAKE AND ATTACH THE PATCHWORK STRAP

37 Lay out the 1½" x 24" (3.8 x 61 cm) strips side by side in the order you'd like them to be. Begin stitching the strips together by placing 2 of them right sides together, matching up all edges; pin and then stitch together along one long side. Press the seam allowances open. Continue adding strips in this manner until you have an 8-strip panel measuring 8½" (21.5 cm) wide.

28 Use a rotary cutter and acrylic ruler (use the side of the ruler as a guide to make straight cuts) to cut the panel across the width (**figure 5**) into 12 units, each measuring 2" x 8½" (3.8 x 16.5 cm).

29 Stitch each strip end to end by placing 2 of them right sides together and stitching along one short end. Continue adding strips in this manner until you have used all the strips, forming 1 long 2" x 96½" (3.8 x 169 cm) strip (**figure 6**).

30 Fold over each short edge ½" (1.3 cm), toward the wrong side, and press. Then, fold over each long edge ½" (1.3 cm), toward the wrong side, and press. Now, fold the strap in half lengthwise, wrong sides together, so that the raw edges are encased inside; press. Edgestitch (p. 154) along the entire length of the strap (at the matched edges) to finish. Go slowly to keep your stitching even.

31 With the back of the pillowcase facing up, find the center of the back panel that is on the opposite side from the embellishments on the front and mark. Fold your strap in half widthwise to find the center. Place the center point of the strap directly over the mark just made on the pillowcase so that the strap runs vertically, parallel to the topstitched hems of the back panels; pin in place. Place the pillowcase on the sewing machine so that the panel with the strap is the only layer that will be sewn, keeping all other fabric out of the way of the needle. Topstitch a short line along the strap to secure it to the pillow (remember to backtack [p. 154]).

COVER AND ATTACH THE BUTTONS

32 Use the cotton print scraps to cover the coverable buttons according to manufacturer's instructions.

33 Use a water-soluble fabric pen to mark the button placement on the bottom panel at the back of the pillow by marking directly through the center of each buttonhole.

34 Sew on the buttons over the marks. Now, insert the pillow form into the finished cover and button the back panels. Wrap the straps around the pillow a few times, tying them in a bow in the front (see the photo on p. 87).

finished size

25" (63.5 cm) long x 15½"
(39.5 cm) wide (lying flat)

materials

Linen *(shown: natural)*

10" x 25½" (5.54 x 65 cm)
rectangle for top

3" x 25½" (7.5 x 65 cm) strip
for top

2 strips, each 2" x 2½"
(5 x 6.5 cm) for loops

Various cotton prints *(7 different
prints shown)*

7 strips, each 1" x 25½" (2.5
x 65 cm) for stripes (cut one
from each of the 7 prints)

16" x 25½" (40 x 65 cm)
rectangle for lining

6 strips, each 1½" x 16½" (3.8 x
42 cm) for patchwork strap

Low-loft batting

16" x 25½" (40 x 65 cm)
rectangle

4 extra large size ⁷⁄₁₆" (1.1 cm)
grommets

tools

Setter and anvil (purchase
these as a set with your
grommets)

Hammer

Point turner (optional)

Walking foot for sewing
machine

Blind hem or edgestitch foot
for sewing machine (optional)

Hera marker

I love my sewing machine dearly and making sure it's clean and dust-free are top on my list. There are also those very rare moments that I like to cover up my machine and put it away for awhile, but I've never been a fan of the covers that usually come with a machine. This appealing cover is the perfect replacement, featuring grommets and a patchwork tie to keep the cover in place with a stylish twist.

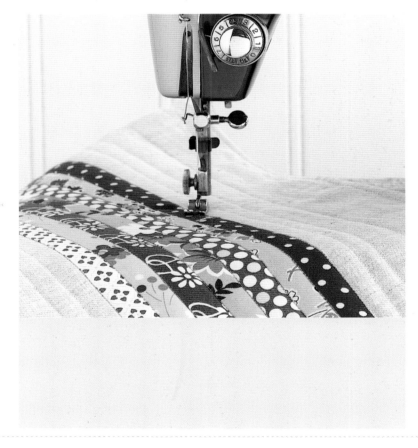

Sewing Machine Cover

Note: All seam allowances are ¼" (6 mm) unless otherwise indicated.

ASSEMBLE THE STRIPES

1 Begin stitching the cotton stripes together by placing 2 of them right sides together, matching up all edges; pin together along one long side. Stitch together along the pinned edge. Continue adding more stripes to the 2-stripe unit just created in the same manner until all 7 stripes are attached to form a panel measuring 3½" (9 cm) wide (**figure 1**). Press all seam allowances open.

ASSEMBLE THE COVER

See the diagram at far right for assistance with the following steps.

2 Place the stripe panel on a flat surface with the right side facing up. Place the 3½" x 25½" (9 x 65 cm) linen strip on top of the stripe panel, right side down, matching up all the edges. Pin and then stitch together along one long side.

3 Open out the panels and lay flat with the right side facing up. Place the 10" x 25½" (25.5 x 65 cm) linen piece on top of the stripe panel, right side down, aligning the pieces at one long edge. Pin and then stitch together. Press the entire piece flat. You now have the completed top.

4 Layer the batting, the completed top (right side up), and the cotton lining (right side down) in that order. Pin the layers together around the perimeter.

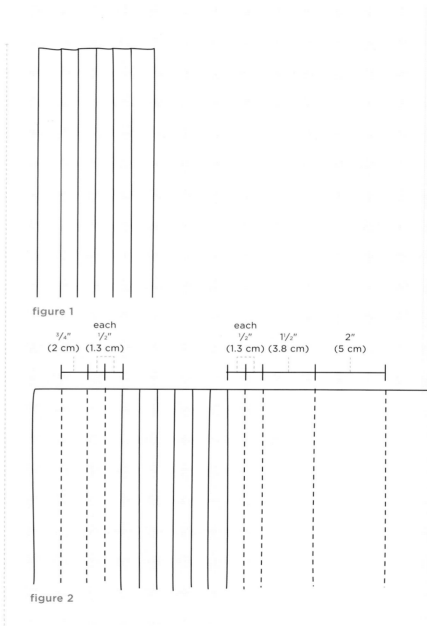

figure 1

figure 2

customizing the cover

Sewing machines come in so many different sizes, you'll want to be sure to measure yours and adjust the pattern if necessary.

With a tape measure, measure your machine from the bottom front, over the top, to the bottom back (if your machine has a top-mounted thread spindle be sure to account for the extra height of the spindle). Add ½" (1.3 cm) to this measurement for seam allowance to obtain the length measurement of your cover. The width measurements given should be sufficient for most sewing machines but use your discretion and add to the width of the linen pieces if you desire, remembering to account for ¼" (6 mm) seam allowances.

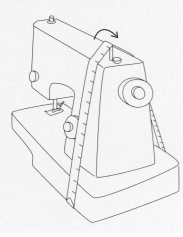

Diagram

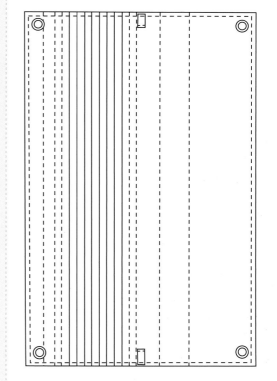

5 Stitch the layers together around the perimeter, leaving a 4" (10 cm) gap for turning.

6 Clip the corners (p. 157). Turn the cover right side out through the gap and push out the corners (use the point turner if necessary).

7 Turn in the seam allowances at the gap and finger press. Topstitch (p. 155) around the perimeter of the cover, about ¼" (6 mm) from the edge.

QUILT THE COVER

8 With the cover lying flat in front of you, right side up, use the hera marker and a ruler to mark guidelines, starting from the stripe panel and using the measurements given in **figure 2**.

9 Using the walking foot and a straight stitch (p. 155), quilt the cover, stitching on the guidelines drawn in Step 8. Quilt the stripe panel by stitching in the ditch (p. 155) between each stripe and at both outer edges of the panel.

CREATE AND ATTACH THE LOOPS

10 Take 1 of the 2″ × 2½″ (5 × 6.5 cm) linen strips and fold it in half lengthwise with right sides together (you now have a piece measuring 1½″ × 2″ [3.8 × 5 cm). Stitch together along the 2″ (5 cm) edge, leaving both sides open to form a tube. Press the seam allowances open, then turn right side out and press flat so that the seam runs down the middle.

11 Fold the seam allowances at each open end inside the tube by ¼″ (6 mm) and press.

12 Repeat Steps 10 and 11 to create the second loop.

13 With the cover facing right side up, pin one loop to the center of each short side (make sure the loop seam faces the cover so it is hidden), placing them vertically about ⅛″ (3 mm) above the edge of the cover. Topstitch the bottom of each loop directly over the previous stitch line, then topstitch the top of each loop about ⅛″ (3 mm) from the edge (see diagram on p. 95).

GROMMETS

14 Placement of the grommets will vary depending on the size of your sewing machine. Before you add the grommets, I suggest placing the cover over your machine

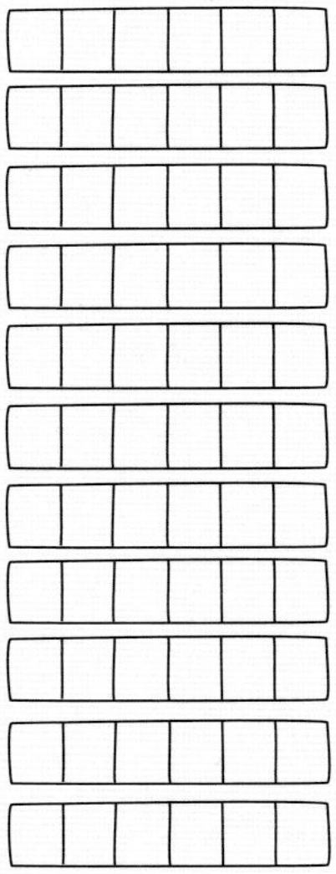

figure 3

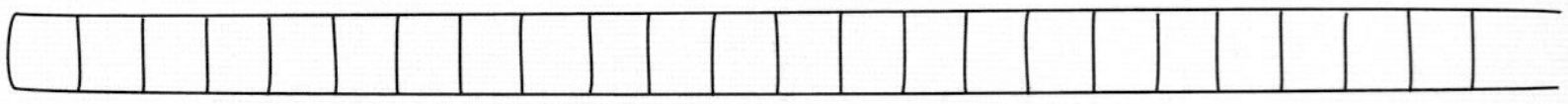

figure 4

to determine the best placement. Be sure that they are not too high for the strap to thread through both the grommets and the loops. Attach one grommet at each corner of the cover according to manufacturer's instructions (be sure to place them at least $1/2"$ [1.3 cm] away from each edge).

MAKE PATCHWORK STRAP

15 Repeat Step 1 on p. 94 to sew the strap pieces ($1^{1}/_{2}" \times 16^{1}/_{2}"$ [3.8 x 42 cm]) together until you have a 6-strip panel measuring $6^{1}/_{2}"$ (16.5 cm) wide.

16 Use a rotary cutter and acrylic ruler (use the side of the ruler as a guide to make straight cuts) to cut the panel across the width into 11 units, each measuring $1^{1}/_{2}" \times 6^{1}/_{2}"$ (3.8 x 16.5 cm; **figure 3**).

17 Stitch each strip end to end by placing 2 of them right sides together and stitching along one short end. Continue adding strips in this manner until you have used all the strips, forming 1 long $1^{1}/_{2}" \times 66^{1}/_{2}"$ (3.8 x 169 cm) strap (**figure 4**).

18 Fold over each short edge of the strap by $1/2"$ (1.3 cm), toward the wrong side, and press. Then, fold over each long edge by $3/8"$ (1 cm), toward the wrong side, and press. Now, fold the strap in half lengthwise, wrong sides together, so that the raw edges are encased inside; press. Edgestitch (p. 154) along the entire length of the strap (at the matched edges) to finish. Go slowly to keep your stitching even. Lace the strap through the grommets and loops, place the cover over the machine, and tie the ends of the strap into a pretty bow!

materials

Linen *(shown: white)*

4" x 6½" (10 x 16.5 cm) rectangle for lining

8" x 6½" (20.5 x 16.5 cm) rectangle for lining

15½" x 6½" (39.5 x 16.5 cm) rectangle for shell

Various cotton prints *(4 different prints shown)*

4 strips, each 1½" x 6½" (3.8 x 16.5 cm) for stripes

Timtex or firm stabilizer

15" x 6" (38 x 15 cm)

Sheer/lightweight fusible interfacing

15½" x 6½" (39.5 x 16.5 cm) rectangle

Embroidery thread

tools

Hera marker (optional)

utensil BASKET

If you're anything like me, having little get-togethers with lots of friends, family, and food is something you love to do. This neat little basket will come in handy for holding utensils on the buffet table. It's simple to make and will add a personalized touch to your table.

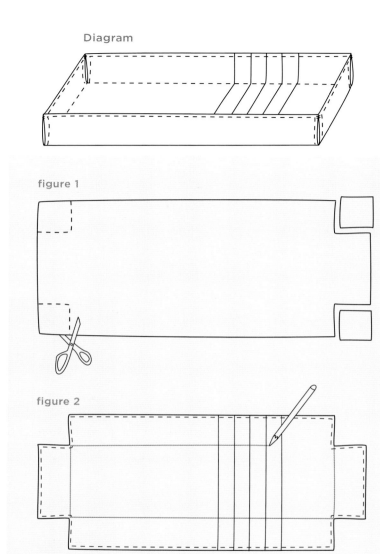

Diagram

figure 1

figure 2

Utensil Basket

Note: All seam allowances are ¼" (6 mm) unless otherwise indicated.

ASSEMBLE THE STRIPES

1 Lay out your 4 (1½" x 6½" [3.8 x 16.5 cm]) stripes in the order you'd like them to appear on the basket.

2 Place 2 of the stripes right sides together, aligning all edges and pin along one long side. Stitch along the pinned length. Repeat entire step with the 2 remaining stripes so that you have 2 units of 2 stripes each.

3 Place the 2 units right sides together, aligning all edges, and pin together along one long side. Stitch along the pinned length. Press all seam allowances to the right.

ASSEMBLE BASKET LINING

See the diagram above for assistance with the following steps.

4 Pin the 4" x 6½" (10 x 16.5 cm) linen lining piece and the assembled stripe piece right sides together, aligning the 6½" (16.5 cm) edges. Stitch the pieces together along the pinned edge. Remove the pins.

5 Pin the 8" x 6½" (20.5 x 16.5 cm) linen lining piece to the opposite edge of the stripes; pin and then stitch as before. Press both sets of seam allowances to the right.

ASSEMBLE THE LAYERS

6 With an acrylic ruler and a water-soluble fabric marking pen or tailor's chalk, mark a

1½" (3.8 cm) square on each corner of the linen shell (15½" x 6½" [39.5 x 16.5 cm]), the assembled lining piece, the fusible interfacing, and the Timtex. Cut out all the squares (**figure 1**).

7 Center the Timtex on the wrong side of the linen shell so that the seam allowances of the shell are left free. Place the fusible interfacing fusible side down on top of the Timtex and linen shell, aligning the edges of the fusible interfacing and linen shell. Fuse according to manufacturer's instructions. This will fix the Timtex in place.

8 Lay the lining piece and linen shell right sides together, aligning the edges, and pin the layers together.

9 Stitch around the edges, through all the layers, pivoting at the corners with the needle still down for a continuous stitch line (see Sewing a Corner on p. 18 for assistance). Stop stitching at least 3" (7.5 cm) before your starting point to leave a gap for turning.

10 Turn the basket right side out through the opening and press.

11 Turn in the seam allowances of the opening by ¼" (6 mm) and finger press, then handstitch closed with a slip stitch (p. 156). Topstitch (p. 155) around the outer edge of the basket, about ¼" (6 mm) from the edge. Press again to make sure the seams lie flat.

12 With the right side (with the stripes) of your basket facing up, use the fabric marking pen or tailor's chalk (or a hera marker if you prefer) and an acrylic ruler to lightly

mark out the bottom of your basket. To do this, mark a rectangle that connects the inner corners (**figure 2**), keeping the lines straight and parallel to the edges (the lines will be 1" [2.5 cm] in from the edges).

13 Topstitch along the lines made in Step 13.

FINISHING

14 Fold the basket sides over, toward the right side (with the stripes) along the topstitched lines and press to set the crease.

15 With your embroidery thread and handsewing needle, tack the basket sides together at the corners with a whipstitch (p. 157) near the top edge (see diagram at top left and the photo on p. 99). Make a knot on the inside of the basket, clip your thread, and you're done!

finished size

11" (28 cm) wide x 12"
(30.5 cm) long (not including
hanging loop)

materials

Linen
>
> 1 rectangle 11½" x 8¾"
> (29 x 22 cm) for calendar front
>
> 1 rectangle 11½" x 12½"
> (29 x 31.5 cm) for calendar back
>
> 7 scraps, each at least 2" x 2"
> (5 x 5 cm) for covering buttons

Various cotton prints (*13 different prints shown*)
>
> 4 strips, each 3¾" x 2" (9.5 x
> 5 cm) for border (A)
>
> 2 strips, each 5" x 2" (12.5 x 5
> cm) for border (B)
>
> 1 strip 11½" x 1¼" (29 x 3.2 cm)
> for border (C)
>
> 31 scraps, each at least 2" x 2"
> (5 x 5 cm) for coverering buttons

Low-loft batting
>
> 1 rectangle, 11½" x 12½" (29 x
> 31.5 cm)

30" (76 cm) of ¾" (2 cm) wide
linen twill tape

11" (28 cm) of cotton cording

Matching sewing thread

Coverable buttons (see Tip on
p. 104); thirty-one ⅞" (2.2 cm)
and seven ¾" (2 cm)

Nonsticky-back Velcro coins;
35 hooks and 35 loops

Nonsticky-back 2½" (6.5 cm)
Velcro strips; 1 hook and 12
loops

Velcro Glue-On Adhesive or
Fabri-Tac glue

1 extra large size ⅞" (2.2 cm)
grommet

CONTINUED ON NEXT PAGE

button CALENDAR

The inspiration for this project came to me in the middle of night, and I had to jump right out of bed to get to work. The resulting adjustable calendar makes me wild with delight because it incorporates some of my favorite things: patchwork, quilting, covering buttons, and stamping. You can practically use this calendar forever, instead of buying a new disposable one every year. If you'd like some variety, just whip up another one in different colors!

tools

Button cover kit

Hera marker

Letter and number stamps sets and black ink pad (recommended: Versa Craft)

Walking foot for sewing machine

X-Acto knife or box cutter

Grommet setter and anvil (purchase these as a kit with your grommets)

Point turner (optional)

TIP

There are coverable buttons available without a hook on the back, called "flat back" coverable buttons. They are perfect for this project. If you can't find these, however, the regular ones will do just fine. You'll just have to remove all of the hooks with a pair of pliers by squeezing the hooks with the pliers and giving them a good turn. They should pop right off.

Button Calendar

Notes: All seam allowances are ¼" (6 mm) unless otherwise indicated.

+ Label the various pieces listed under Materials on p. 103, using a water-soluble fabric pen or tailor's chalk and marking on the wrong side of the fabric. This will make identification easier as you sew. If the marks show through to the right side of the fabric, be sure to remove them with water or as directed by the manufacturer as you go.

+ It is important to choose an ink pad that is specifically for stamping on fabric, like Versa Craft, which dries quickly and becomes permanent when ironed.

PREPARE THE BUTTONS

1 Cover all of the buttons according to the manufacturer's instructions. Cover all of the ¾" (2 cm) buttons with the linen scraps and all of the ⅞" (2.2 cm) buttons with the cotton scraps. If the buttons you

have are the type with the hooks on the back, now is a good time to remove them.

2 Turn all of your covered buttons wrong side up. Add a few drops of glue on the back of a covered button and press one of the Velcro loop coins onto the center of the button over the glue (make sure the "loops" are facing up). Repeat to attach a Velcro loop coin to the back of each button. Set aside to dry.

3 Once the glue has dried, arrange the large buttons in front of you in the order you'd like them to be on the calendar. One by one, carefully stamp each button with a number (1–31) using the number stamps and black ink pad. Set them aside to dry.

PREPARE THE CALENDAR FRONT

4 With a hera marker and an acrylic ruler, mark out the grid on the calendar front, according to **figure 1** on p. 107.

5 Before completing this step, you may want to do a few practice stamps on some

Diagram

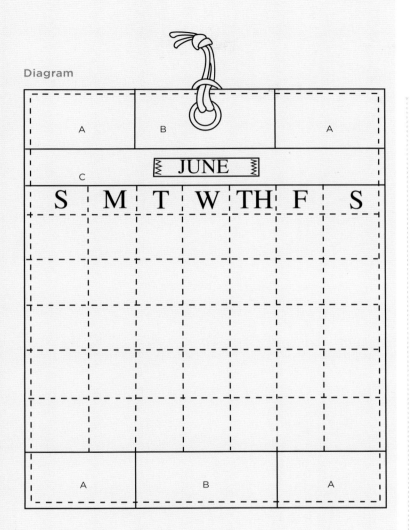

fabric scraps. In the top 1" (2.5 cm) grid spaces, stamp a letter to represent the day of the week in each space, (S, M, T, W, TH, F, S—left to right; see the diagram) with the letter stamps and black ink pad. Keep the letters centered and about ¹/₈" (3 mm) above the bottom grid line of the space (**figure 2** on p. 107).

6 Place a Velcro hook coin at the middle of each remaining space on the grid (even though the coins have nonsticky backs, the backs will still have a light amount of adhesive that will help the coins stay put until you sew them).

7 Zigzag stitch (p. 155) back and forth over each Velcro coin a few times. You can lift the needle and move on to the next coin without clipping threads to save time, then clip all the threads between the Velcro coins once you're done. Set aside the calendar front.

8 On the linen twill tape, measure and mark (use the fabric marking pen) a vertical line, every 2¹/₂" (6.5 cm) along the length. You will have 12 segments, each measuring 2¹/₂" (6.5 cm). Use the letter stamps and black ink pad to stamp each segment with one of the twelve months of the year (January–December) so that you have a complete twelve-month set. Try to keep the lettering centered on each segment. You may want to practice on a scrap first. Cut apart the segments at the lines.

9 Place a Velcro loop strip on the back of each segment of twill tape and zigzag stitch over each edge of the twill tape, through both layers, to secure the Velcro and prevent fraying.

ASSEMBLE THE CALENDAR BORDER

See the diagram on p. 105 for assistance with assembly.

10 Place 1 of the A border strips on top of 1 of the B border strips with right sides together, lining up all the edges. Stitch together along one of the short (2″ [5 cm] edges. Press the seam allowances open and then press the piece flat.

11 Repeat Step 10 to attach another A border strip to the opposite side of the B border strip, create 1 strip measuring 11½″ (29 cm) long.

12 Repeat Steps 10 and 11 with the remaining B strip and 2 A strips. You now have 2 completed borders.

13 Lay the C border strip on top of 1 of the completed borders with right sides together, lining up one long edge. Pin together and then stitch along the long edge. Press the seam allowances open and press the piece flat.

14 Now, take the border unit you just created and align the 11½″ (29 cm) edge of the C strip (added in Step 13) with the top edge of the calendar front, with right sides together (above the stamped days of the week). Pin together and then stitch along the edge. Press the seam allowances up toward the border.

15 Finally, lay the second border on top of the calendar front, right sides together, aligning the long edge of the border with the bottom edge of the calendar front. Pin and then stitch together along the bottom edge. Press the seam allowances down toward the border.

16 Stitch the Velcro loop strip to the center of the C strip of the top border, using a zigzag stitch at each end.

ASSEMBLE AND QUILT THE CALENDAR

17 Layer the pieces in this order: batting, calendar front (right side up), calendar back (right side down).

18 Align all of the edges and pin around the perimeter to keep the layers from shifting.

19 Using a walking foot, stitch around the perimeter through all of the layers, leaving at least a 3″ (7.5 cm) opening to turn.

20 Clip the corners (p. 157) and turn the calendar inside out through the opening. Poke out the corners, using a point turner or other pointed object such as a knitting needle, if necessary; press.

21 Turn in the seam allowances at the opening by ¼″ (6 mm) and handstitch closed using a slip stitch (p. 156).

22 Following the grid lines you created earlier on the calendar front, machine quilt the

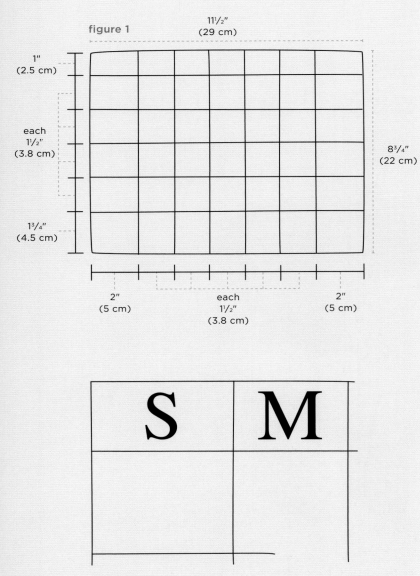

figure 1

11½"
(29 cm)

1"
(2.5 cm)

each
1½"
(3.8 cm)

1¾"
(4.5 cm)

8¾"
(22 cm)

2"
(5 cm)

each
1½"
(3.8 cm)

2"
(5 cm)

S M

figure 2

calendar through all three layers by using a straight stitch (p. 155), adjusting the stitch length to 1/16" (2 mm) for the beginning and ending ¼' (6 mm) of each stitch line. Machine quilt directly on top of the horizontal seam on the top border in the same manner. Finally, machine quilt around the perimeter of the calendar, ⅛"–¼" (3–6 mm) from the edge, turning at the corners without lifting the needle for a continuous stitch line (use the regular stitch length for this entire stitch line).

23 Mark the center top of your calendar with the fabric marking pen exactly where you'd like to place the grommet. Place the "male" side of the grommet on the calendar front over the mark and trace the inside of the grommet with the fabric marking pen or tailor's chalk. Cut out the hole using an X-Acto knife.

24 Assemble the grommet according to manufacturer's instructions.

25 Fold the cotton cording in half and tie an overhand knot (p. 156) at the end with both tails held together.

26 Insert the looped end through the front of the grommet and bring it around to the top of the calendar. Pass the knotted end through the loop and pull all the way through (see diagram on p. 105 for assistance).

Frame measures about 10½" x 10½" (26.5 x 26.5 cm) when fully extended. Mobile hangs about 18" (45.5 cm) long from the top of the frame (not including hanging loop).

materials

Sport weight (#2 Fine) linen yarn *(shown: Euroflax Sport Weight in #36 natural)*

Various cotton prints *(14 different prints shown)*

   4 different print rectangles, each 17" x 8" (43 x 20.5 cm) for flowers

   2 different print rectangles, each 10" x 4" (25.5 x 10 cm) for large leaves

   2 different print rectangles, each 8" x 3" (20.5 x 7.5 cm) for small leaves

   4" x 4" (10 x 10 cm) square for tied "scrap leaves"

   8 different print scraps, each at least 3" x 3" (7.5 x 7.5 cm) for yo-yo flowers

   4 scraps, each at least 2" x 2" (5 x 5 cm) for covering buttons

Batting

   4 squares, each 4" x 4" (10 x 10 cm) for large leaves

   4 squares, each 3" x 3" (7.5 x 7.5 cm) for small leaves

18" (45.5 cm) of ¾" (2 cm) wide linen ribbon *(shown: natural)*

4 size 30 (¾" [2 cm]) coverable buttons

Double-stick fusible web (recommended: Steam-a-Seam2)

24" (61 cm) of 10- or 12-gauge florist stem wire or craft wire

Permanent fabric adhesive (recommended: Fabri-tac)

Fray Check (optional)

Paper or card stock for templates

CONTINUED ON NEXT PAGE

flower MOBILE

Do you know a little girl who loves flowers? Well now she can have beautiful flowers all year-round with this fun-to-make mobile. Mix and match the flowers and colors to create your own special "bouquet." This eye-catching mobile will be right at home hanging over a crib or a child's bed for a sweet decoration with an organic sensibility.

Flower Mobile templates
(pp. 150 and 151)

Awl

Darning needle

Needle-nose pliers

Point turner (optional)

Blind hem or edgestitch foot
for sewing machine (optional)

Flower Mobile

1 Trace the Flower Mobile templates onto paper or card stock (card stock will create a sturdier template). Cut out all templates and set aside.

CREATE THE FLOWERS

2 Take the 4 cotton print pieces for the flowers (17″ x 8″ [43 x 20.5 cm]) and, with a rotary cutter and an acrylic ruler, cut each in half widthwise so that you have eight 8½″ x 4″ (21.5 x 10 cm) pieces (use the edge of the ruler as a guide to make straight cuts).

3 Take one half of each print and set them in front of you, wrong side up; set aside the other halves for now. Iron the fusible web to the wrong side of the halves in front of you. Allow them to cool for a minute and then remove the paper backing.

4 Next, pair the prints with the fusible web to the matching halves of the prints you set aside earlier. Place each pair wrong

sides together, matching up all edges and then iron them together; let cool.

5 Now you're going to trace a flower template set onto one side of each of the print pieces created in Steps 2–4 with a water-soluble fabric pen or tailor's chalk (use each set of templates twice or as desired).

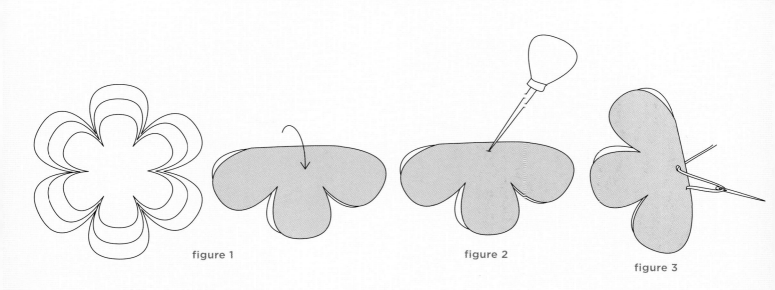

figure 1

figure 2

figure 3

6 With sharp scissors, carefully cut out all of your flowers.

7 Spray or dab any remaining pen marks with water to remove them and iron to dry. It may take a few sprays to completely remove the markings.

8 You can dab a little Fray Check around the edges of the flowers, if desired, but the fusible web should stop the fabric from fraying.

ASSEMBLE THE FLOWERS

9 First, cover the 4 buttons with the cotton print scraps (2" x 2" [5 x 5 cm]) according to manufacturer's instructions and then set them aside.

10 Layer 1 set of flowers together with the largest flower on the bottom and the smallest flower on top. Holding them together, fold them in half, enveloping the small and medium flower inside the large one (**figure 1**).

11 Lay the folded set of flowers down onto your self-healing mat and with your awl make a hole through the middle of the flowers, near the folded edge (**figure 2**). Push the awl through a little to make sure the hole is big enough for two strands of yarn to pass through. This may take a little force. Put your back into it! This side is now the back of the flower.

12 Thread the darning needle with a short length of yarn and set aside. Unfold 1 of the flower sets and, with the right side facing up, place 1 of the covered buttons in the center, placing the shank into the crease, between the holes. Pass the threaded darning needle through the holes from the back, passing through the button shank in the center (**figure 3**). Remove the needle and tie a secure double overhand knot (p. 156) with the two ends of your yarn. You can add some Fabri-tac or other permanent fabric adhesive to the knot, if desired, to make sure it is secure.

13 Repeat Steps 10–12 with the 3 remaining flower sets; set aside.

CREATE THE YO-YO FLOWERS

14 Thread the handsewing needle with a strand of thread and knot both ends together (p. 17) so that the thread is doubled and set aside for use in Step 16. Use the water-soluble fabric marker cr tailor's chalk to trace the yo-yo template onto the wrong side of each of the yo-yo cotton print scraps (at least 3″ x 3″ [7.5 x 7.5 cm]) and cut them out. You will have 8 circles.

15 Fold over the edges of a yo-yo piece about ¼″ (6 mm), toward the wrong side, and finger press (p. 154).

16 Handstitch around the edge of the yo-yo, using a running stitch and leaving a thread tail. Stitch close to the edge, making small, even stitches (you'll probably have to re-fold the edge along the crease as you stitch). Work your way around the entire circle until you're back where you started. Do not tie off.

17 Once you've finished stitching, pull the thread tails to make the gathers of your yo-yo (**figure 4**), then continue gathering the edges into a tight circle. Spread the gathers evenly and make an overhand knot (p. 156) to secure the tails, then trim the threads. Flatten out the yo-yo.

18 Repeat Steps 15–17 with each of the remaining yo-yo pieces and then set them aside.

CREATE THE LEAVES

19 Use the leaf templates cut out earlier and a water-soluble fabric pen cr tailor's chalk to trace four large leaves onto the wrong side of each of the 10″ x 4″ (25.5 x 10 cm) cotton print rectangles. With sharp scissors, carefully cut all of your leaves. Repeat entire step to trace four small leaves onto each of the 8″ x 3″ (20.5 x 7.5 cm) cotton print rectangles. Arrange the leaves large leaves into pairs as desired so each leaf has a front and back, repeat to pair small leaves.

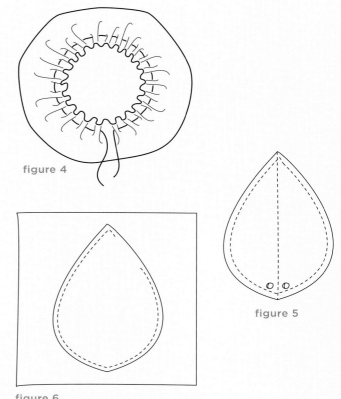

figure 4

figure 5

figure 6

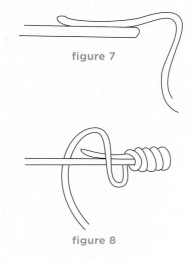

figure 7

figure 8

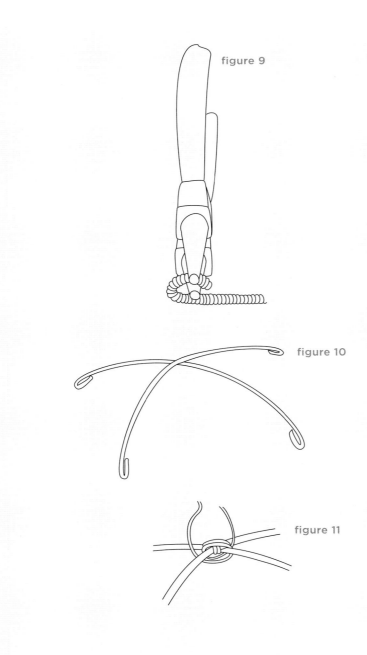

figure 9

figure 10

figure 11

ASSEMBLE THE LEAVES

20 With the 4" x 4" (10 x 10 cm) batting squares, layer each large leaf in the following order: batting, leaf front (right side up), leaf back (right side down); make sure the leaves are centered on the batting and pin the layers together.

21 Stitch around each leaf, about ¼" (6 mm) from the edge, leaving a gap wide enough for turning near the tip of the leaf (to one side of the tip; **figure 5**). Trim the batting all the way around the leaves, in line with the edge of the leaf. Clip off the points at the top and bottom of the leaf as you would a corner (p. 157) and clip along the curves (p. 157).

22 Turn each leaf inside out and push out the tips (use the point tuner if necessary).

23 On each leaf, fold in the seam allowances at the gap and handstitch closed with a slip stitch (p. 156).

24 Repeat Steps 20–23 with the small leaves and the 3" x 3" (7.5 x 7.5 cm) batting squares.

QUILT THE LEAVES

25 Edgestitch (p. 154) around the edge of each leaf, pivoting at the corners without lifting the needle for a continuous stitch line (see **figure 6**).

26 Embellish each leaf by quilting as desired. Try topstitching down the center of each leaf (**figure 6**). You could also add diagonal lines of stitching running from the center stitch line to create the veins of the leaf. It's completely up to you, have fun with it! You now have the completed leaves—four large and four small.

27 Lay your leaves down on the self-healing mat and use your awl to make two holes through each near the bottom, large enough for one strand of yarn to pass through snugly (see **figure 6** for hole placement). Set leaves aside.

PREPARE THE SCRAP LEAVES

28 This part is super easy! Simply take the 4" x 4" (10 x 10 cm) cotton print square and use the rotary cutter and acrylic ruler to cut it into four 1" x 4" (2.5 x 10 cm) strips (use the edge of the ruler as a guide to make straight cuts). You'll tie these onto the mobile after it's assembled; set aside.

WRAP THE WIRES

29 Cut the 24" (61 cm) piece of wire in half.

30 Place about 1" (2.5 cm) of the yarn onto one end of one of the wires and add a few drops of fabric adhesive to secure (**figure 7**). Give it a few minutes to dry.

31 Start wrapping the yarn around the wire, beginning at the edge of the wire and wrapping over the 1" (2.5 cm) tail that is glued down. Be sure to wrap the yarn tightly and with no space left between wraps (**figure 8**).

32 Continue winding the yarn tightly around the wire all the way to the other end. When you get to the end tie a secure overhand knot (p. 156) through the previous wrap and add a few drops of fabric adhesive to the knot. Allow the glue to dry completely, then clip the tail of the yarn as close to the knot as possible.

33 With the pliers, turn each end of the wrapped wire under about $3/4$" (2 cm), forming a hook. To do this, hold the wire firmly in one hand and grasp the end of the wire with the pliers, about 1" (2.5 cm) from the edge, and begin to turn the wire

downward. Then, use your finger to continue pushing the wire around the pliers until you have formed a hook shape (**figure 9**).

34 Repeat Steps 30–33 with the remaining wire.

ASSEMBLE THE MOBILE FRAME

35 Once the glue has dried completely, make an "X" with the two wrapped wires, making sure that all the hooks are facing down (**figure 10**).

36 Take a long piece of yarn and place the center of it underneath the "X."

37 Pick up the two ends of the yarn and wrap the yarn around the "X" looping around one side of the "X" and then around the other. Wrap tightly in this manner about three or four times to make sure the wires stay in place (**figure 11**). Holding both yarn tails together, tie a loose overhand knot (p. 156) at the top of the wires, then snug the knot up against the wires and tighten the knot securely. Add a drop of fabric adhesive to the knot and allow to dry completely. Trim one of the tails close to the knot, leaving the remaining tail in place. Tie a loop at the end of the remaining tail for hanging the mobile.

ASSEMBLE THE MOBILE VINES

See the Diagram at right for assistance with the following steps.

38 Cut 4 pieces of linen yarn, each about 16" (40.5 cm) long; set aside. Gather all of your flowers and leaves and make 4 groups (1 group will hang from each side of the mobile so group the colors as desired), each consisting of:

> 1 flower, 1 large leaf, 1 small leaf, 2 yo-yo flowers, 1 scrap leaf (1" x 4" [2.5 x 10 cm] strip).

39 Thread the darning needle with one of the pieces of yarn. With 1 of the groups made in Step 38 in front of you, start with the large flower and, leaving a yarn tail a

Diagram

few inches long, run the needle through both holes made earlier (next to the yarn securing the button to the flower); tie an overhand knot to secure the flower in place (you may need to make a double or triple overhand knot to prevent the flower from sliding down).

40 Now, take the large leaf and run the needle through both holes made earlier as before (do not tie a knot). Next, take 1 of your yo-yos and pass the needle through the back of it, only picking up the back fabric. Repeat entire step with the small leaf and the remaining yo-yo.

41 Remove the needle from the yarn and tie an overhand knot at the end of the yarn (this is now the bottom of the "vine").

42 Slide the last yo-yo down onto the knot and tie the scrap leaf onto the yarn just above the yo-yo.

43 Repeat Steps 39–42 with the remaining groups so that you have 4 "vines."

44 Tie a "vine" securely to each of the hooks on the mobile frame created earlier, using the yarn tail near the flower; trim any excess yarn tail from the top of the vine.

45 Spread the yo-yos and leaves out evenly or as desired, along the yarn. Use the linen ribbon to tie a pretty bow around the yarn just above the mobile frame. Cut the ends of the ribbon at an angle. Hang up your mobile and enjoy!

About 7 ½" (19 cm) long (end to end) x 2 ½" (6.5 cm) deep x 2" (5 cm) wide

materials

Linen *(shown: natural)*

5 strips, each 8½" x 1½" (21.5 x 3.8 cm) for shell A panels

2 strips, each 8½" x ¾" (21.5 x 2 cm) for shell B panels

2 scraps, each at least 2½" x 3" (6.5 x 7.5 cm) for large hexagons

Various cotton prints *(4 different prints shown)*

3 strips, each 8½" x 1½" (21.5 x 3.8 cm) for lining A panels

2 strips, each 8½" x 2" (21.5 x 5 cm) for lining B panels

2 scraps, each at least 2½" x 3" (6.5 x 7.5 cm) for large hexagons

2 scraps, each 1½" x 1½" (3.8 x 3.8 cm) for pull-tab

8 scraps, each at least 1½" x 1½" (3.8 x 3.8 cm) for mini hexagons

2 strips, each 1½" x 1" (3.8 x 2.5 cm) for zipper tabs

2 strips, each 1¾" x 1½" (4.5 x 3.8 cm) for zipper loops

Heavyweight fusible interfacing

5 strips, each 8" x 1" (21.5 x 3.8 cm)

2 strips, each 8" x ¾" (21.5 x 2 cm)

2 scraps, each at least 2½" x 3" (6.5 x 7.5 cm) for large hexagons

¾" (2 cm) round button

7" (18 cm) standard zipper

CONTINUED ON NEXT PAGE

pencil CASE

I truly enjoy English Paper Piecing, the popular technique that was my inspiration for this pencil case. The hexagon shapes thrill me to bits—I'd put them on everything if I could, and so this tubular hexagon-shaped bag was born. Add a colorful flower with hexagon petals as embellishment and you have a lovely little case for pencils or whatever else you like!

Small scrap of linen yarn for pull-tab (about 2½" [6.5 cm] long)

Paper or card stock for templates

Silk thread for paper piecing (optional)

tools

Large and Mini Hexagon templates (p. 151)

Zipper foot for sewing machine

Blind hem or edgestitch foot for sewing machine (optional)

Copy machine (optional)

Pencil Case

Notes: All seam allowances are ¼" (6 mm) unless otherwise indicated.

+ Label the various pieces listed under Materials on p. 117, using a water-soluble fabric pen or tailor's chalk and marking on the wrong side of the fabric. This will make identification easier as you sew. If the marks show through to the right side of the fabric, be sure to remove them with water or as directed by the manufacturer, as you go.

1 Copy or trace the Large Hexagon template onto paper or card stock (card stock makes a sturdier template) and cut out. Repeat to create 8 Mini Hexagon templates (I suggest using paper for these instead of card stock). Set all templates aside for now.

ASSEMBLE THE ZIPPER PANEL

2 Take 2 of the cotton print zipper tab pieces and fold each in half widthwise, with wrong sides together, and press. Each

of these pieces will now measure about ¾" x 1" (2 x 2.5 cm).

3 Place the folded edge of one zipper tab on each short end of the zipper, placing the folded edge just to the outside of the zipper stops. The zipper should now measure 8½" (21.5 cm) long from the end of one zipper tab to the end of the opposite zipper tab (you can adjust the placement of the zipper tabs slightly, if necessary, to achieve the proper length). Edgestitch (p. 154) the tabs in place along the folded edges (**figure 1**).

4 Following manufacturer's instructions, fuse the 8" x ¾" (20.5 x 2 cm) interfacing strips to the wrong sides of the shell B panels (centered along the length so that ¼" [6 mm] of linen is left free on each short side of the B panel). Then, fold one long side of each of the panels toward the wrong side by ¼" (6 mm) and press.

5 Place one B panel, right side up, on top of the zipper tape on one side of the zipper, with the folded edge of the zipper panel

figure 1

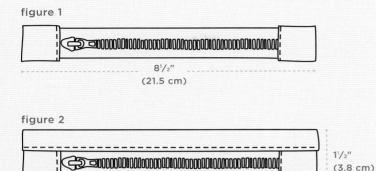

8½"
(21.5 cm)

figure 2

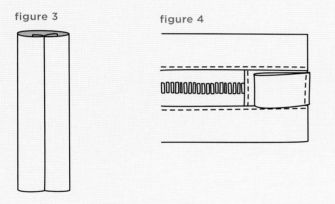

1½"
(3.8 cm)

figure 3

figure 4

figure 5

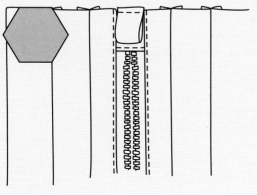

about ¼" (6 mm) from the zipper teeth. Pin in place. Repeat to place the remaining zipper panel on the opposite zipper tape. Your assembled zipper panel should be 8½" (21.5 cm) long x 1½" (3.8 cm) wide, so adjust the placement of the B panels if necessary. Using your zipper foot, edgestitch the B panels in place (**figure 2**); set the completed zipper panel aside.

ASSEMBLE THE PENCIL CASE

6 Following manufacturer's instructions, fuse the 8" x 1" (20.5 x 2.5 cm) interfacing strips, centered, to the wrong sides of the shell A panels (¼" [6 mm] of linen will be left free on all sides of the A panels).

7 Place one of the A panels on top of the completed zipper panel, right sides together, and lining up the 8½" (21.5 cm) edges; pin together. Stitch together along the pinned edge.

8 Repeat Step 8 to add another A panel on the opposite side of the zipper panel. Continue adding A panels in this manner until you have 2 on one side of the zipper

english paper piecing

There are so many things that I love about patchwork, but I think I love English Paper Piecing the most of all. The patchwork piecing technique consists of hand piecing the fabric over paper templates. It's completely portable and is a great way to use up some of those fabric scraps you've been hoarding. Although I am using hexagons here, this technique is very versatile and can be used for almost any shape. See the Patchwork Ball on p. 28 for an example of using this technique with triangles.

1 The templates for this project have already been prepared (see Step 1 on p. 118). To prepare shapes for another project, simply create paper templates that are the desired size of the finished pieces. The templates can be made by tracing the shape onto paper or card stock (I prefer paper for this technique as it is easier to stitch around) or copying the templates and then cutting them out, or you can even buy pre-cut shapes (available at many quilt shops).

2 Pin one paper template to the wrong side of the desired fabric scrap and cut around the template, leaving 1/4" (6 mm) seam allowance on all edges (**figure a**).

3 Fold the seam allowance over the template at each edge and begin hand-basting the folded edges together (**figures b–f**). Keep the folded edges neat and the corners crisp, being careful not to sew the fabric to the paper (your stitches should only catch the layers of fabric). You can simply carry the thread along between the corners, there is no need to knot and cut the thread until you have completed the stitching. Complete the last fold and baste it in place, then knot and trim the thread; be sure to remove the pin.

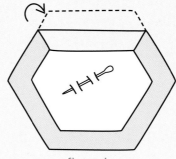

figure b

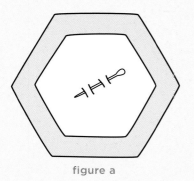

figure a

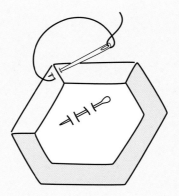

figure c

4 Repeat Steps 2 and 3 with all of the remaining paper templates. To finish the embellishment for this project, follow the stitching instructions below and see Step 17 on p. 124 for instructions on creating the flower shape to embellish the pencil case.

GENERAL STITCHING INSTRUCTIONS TO ATTACH THE SHAPES:

To stitch the shapes together, place 2 of the finished shapes right sides together, aligning them at the edge to be attached. With your needle and thread (I like to use silk thread for this, as it's a finer, stronger thread than cotton, and the stitches are almost invisible), whipstitch (p. 157) the 2 shapes together along the edge, being sure to pick up only two or three threads of the fabric (**figure g**). Using such tiny stitches will keep the stitching virtually invisible. Do not stitch through the paper and try to keep the stitching as close to the edge of the shapes as possible. When you get to a corner make a few extra stitches to reinforce the seam. Once you've finished stitching all the shapes together, press them and then remove the paper templates.

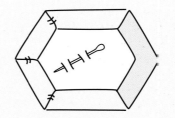

figure e

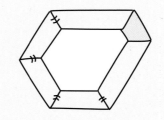

figure f

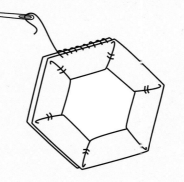

figure g

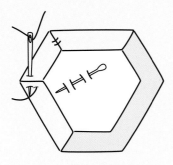

figure d

panel and 3 on the other side. Press all seam allowances open. You now have the assembled pencil case panel.

9 Take the zipper loop pieces and fold each in half lengthwise, with right sides together so that they now measure 1³/₄″ (4.5 cm) long x ³/₄″ (2 cm) wide. Stitch along the long matched edges to form tubes. Press the seam allowances open, then trim them to ¹/₈″ (3 mm). Turn the tubes right side out and press flat so that the seams run down the middle (**figure 3**).

10 Now fold each of the zipper loops in half widthwise and finger press (p. 154).

11 Pin or hand-baste (p. 154) the newly made zipper loops to the assembled pencil case directly over the zipper tabs and lining up the raw edges (**figure 4**).

12 Using the Large Hexagon template (prepared in Step 1), trace and cut 1 large hexagon from each of the linen and interfacing scraps (you will have 2 linen hexagons and 2 interfacing hexagons). Trim ¹/₄″ (6 mm) from each side of the interfacing hexagons only. Then, following manufacturer's instructions, fuse the interfacing hexagons, centered, to the wrong sides of the linen hexagons.

13 Place the assembled pencil case panel flat with the right side facing up and unzip the zipper. Match up one flat side of the hexagon with one edge of an A panel that lies at the outer edge of the assembled pencil case panel (**figure 5**); be sure to align the hexagon with the seam between the 2 A panels (the outer edge of the A panel will hang past the hexagon for seam

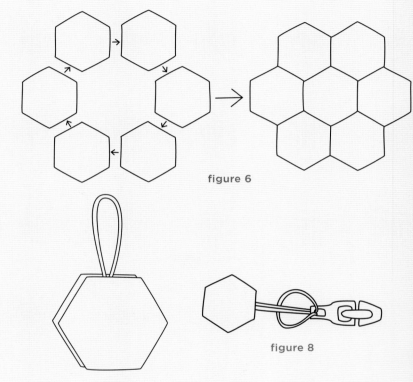

figure 6

figure 7

figure 8

allowance to sew the pencil case closed). Stitch the hexagon and the A panel edges together, leaving the needle down when you come to the first corner. Bring the adjoining flat edge of the hexagon together with the next A panel, pivoting the fabric as you would to sew a corner (p. 18) and sew the next matched edges together. Continue stitching each flat side of the hexagon to the A panels; when you reach the zipper panel, make sure that the zipper loop is lying flat and is sandwiched between the layers. Repeat entire step at the opposite end of the pencil case panel with the remaining large hexagon.

14 Once you have stitched the hexagons to each of the panels, the end panels will be right next to each other. Stitch these together down the long side to complete the case (make sure your zipper is still open!). Trim the seam allowances at each end to $1/8''$ (3 mm) and clip the corners (p. 157) if necessary to allow the seams to lie as flat as possible. Set aside for now.

EMBELLISH THE PENCIL CASE

15 Create 8 mini hexagons using the Mini Hexagon templates, prepared in Step 1 and the cotton print scraps, according to the instructions for English Paper Piecing in the sidebar on pp. 120 and 121.

16 Stitch 6 of the mini hexagons together to form a flower shape, then remove the paper templates and basting stitches, according to the general stitching instructions in the sidebar. See **figure 6** for flower assembly.

17 Position the flower on one side of the pencil case, centering it over one of the long seams (flower shown was positioned on the left side, centered over the second seam below the zipper; see the photo on p. 123). Handsew the flower to the pencil case, using a blindstitch (p. 156) around the outer edges of the flower to secure it to the case.

18 Handsew your button to the center of the flower.

19 Fold the linen yarn in half and place the two remaining mini hexagons over the cut ends, with wrong sides together, so that the ends of the yarn are sandwiched between the hexagons (**figure 7**).

20 Whipstitch the 2 hexagons together around the edges, taking very tiny stitches (pick up only two or three threads of the fabric) to keep them invisible. Be sure to stitch through the yarn as well (where it exits the hexagons) to secure it in place.

21 Slip the end of the looped yarn through the hole in the zipper pull and then pass the hexagon through the loop (**figure 8**) and pull tight to secure the zipper pull-tab in place.

CREATE AND ATTACH THE LINING

22 Place 1 of the lining B panels right sides together with 1 of the lining A panels, aligning them along one 8½" (21.5 cm) edge, and pin. Stitch together along the pinned edge. Add the remaining 2 A panels to the free side of the first A panel in the same manner, then add the remaining B panel so that you have 1 piece, measuring 6½" (16.5 cm) wide, made up of the lining panels in this order: B, A, A, A, B. Press all seam allowances open.

23 Fold over ¼" (6 mm) toward the wrong side on each long edge of the assembled lining and press.

24 Using the Large Hexagon template, trace and cut 2 large hexagons from the cotton print scraps. Then, repeat Step 14 to attach 1 hexagon to each short side of the assembled lining; this time the hexagons will match up without seam allowance hanging past at the edge because you have already folded this under (in Step 23). Stitch right over this fold as you attach the hexagons to secure it in place. Trim the seam allowances at each end to ⅛" (3 mm). You now have the completed lining with one long edge left open. Turn the case right side out.

25 With the shell pencil case still inside out, place it inside of the lining case (wrong sides will be together) so that the opening of the lining case falls along the zipper tape, with the folded-under edges of the lining directly over the place where the shell panel edges are stitched to the zipper tape on the opposite side. Adjust placement as necessary to ensure that the edges of the lining will be about ¼" (6 mm) from the zipper teeth on each side and pin in place.

26 Turn the pencil case inside out. Then, handsew the folded-under lining edges to the zipper tape with a slip stitch (p. 156), being careful not to sew through the shell fabric; remove the pins. If desired, you can

tack the hexagons of the lining and shell together to hold the lining in place; take a few tiny stitches through the seams of the lining and shell at intervals around the hexagon ends of the pencil case, keeping the stitches hidden in the seams. Turn the pencil case right side cut and fill with pencils and pens or other bits and pieces.

materials

Linen (*shown: natural*)
  25¹/₂" x 3¹/₂" (65 x 9 cm) strip

Various cotton prints for log
cabin top (*11 different prints shown,
one for each piece*)

  2 squares, each 1¹/₂" x 1¹/₂"
  (3.8 x 3.8 cm; #1 and #2)

  2 squares, each 1¹/₂" x 2 ¹/₂"
  (3.8 x 6.5 cm; #3 and #4)

  2 rectangles, each 3¹/₂" x 1¹/₂"
  (9 x 3.8 cm; #5 and #6)

  4¹/₂" x 3" (11.5 x 7.5 cm)
  rectangle (#7)

  3" x 1¹/₂" (7.5 x 3.8 cm)
  rectangle (#8)

  5¹/₂" x 3" (14 x 7.5 cm)
  rectangle (#9)

  2 rectangles, each 8¹/₂" x 3"
  (21.5 x 7.5 cm) (#10 and #11)

Cotton print for box lining

  (A) 7³/₄" x 6" (19.5 x 15 cm)
  rectangle

  (B) 6" x 8" (15 x 20.5 cm)
  rectangle

  (C) 2 rectangles, each 2³/₄" x
  7³/₄" (7 x 19.5 cm)

  (D) 2 rectangles, each 2³/₄" x
  5³/₄" (7 x 14.5 cm)

  (E) 6 Ð" x 1¹/₂" (16.8 x 3.8 cm)
  rectangle

Book board (.087 thickness)
  9" x 11" (23 x 28 cm) rectangle

  7¹/₄" x 5¹/₄" (18.5 x 13.5 cm)
  rectangle

Chipboard

  (A) 6³/₄" x 5" (17 x 12.5 cm)
  rectangle

  (B) 5" x 7" (12.5 x 18 cm)
  rectangle

CONTINUED ON NEXT PAGE

fabric covered BOX

I'm always in need of new places to store my growing collection
of sewing sundries (I'm sure I'm not alone), and this pretty box
is a wonderful solution for storing trims, buttons, or other trea-
sures. The technique used here is called *cartonnage*, a traditional
French craft that can be dated back to the nineteenth century.
I've simply updated it to make the process a bit quicker.

(C) 2 rectangles, each 1¾" x 6¾" (4.5 x 17 cm)

(D) 2 rectangles, each 1¾" x 4¾" (4.5 x 12 cm)

Low-loft batting
7¼" x 5¼" (18.5 x 13.5 cm) rectangle

Card stock *(in a solid coordinating color)*
4½" x 6½" (11.5 x 16.5 cm) rectangle

Double-stick fusible web (recommended: Steam-a-Seam2)

tools

PVA (polyvinyl acetate) glue

Small paintbrush

Masking tape

X-Acto knife or box cutter

Bone folder

mitered corners

Use the following instructions to miter the corners on the lid in Step 9 and on the bottom of the box in Step 12:

1 At one corner, pinch the fabric together and clip both sides of the fabric at an angle, toward the corner of the box (you will cut off a triangle-shaped piece of fabric; **figure 1a and 1b**). Don't cut too closely to the corner, as you want to be able to overlap the two edges without having a raw edge exposed at the corner. Repeat pinching and cutting at the remaining corners.

2 With the corners clipped, you can now fold the fabric over the edges of the box. Fold one cut fabric edge over the box, then fold under the adjacent cut edge at the same corner and finger press to create a "finished" edge (**figure 2**).

3 Now fold the adjacent fabric edge over the box, overlapping the raw edge at the corner. You now have a finished mitered corner (**figure 3**). Repeat at the remaining corners.

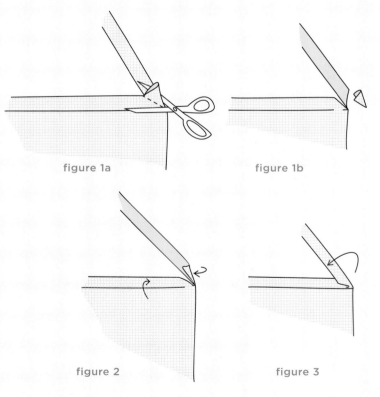

figure 1a

figure 1b

figure 2

figure 3

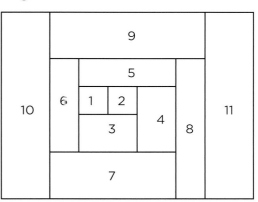

TIP

To keep track of the lettered cotton lining and chipboard pieces (see Materials on pp. 127 and 128) mark them with the indicated letters. Try using tailor's chalk to mark the lining fabric so that you can easily wipe away the marks when they are no longer needed. Using a pencil to mark the chipboard is fine, as these pieces will be covered.

Diagram

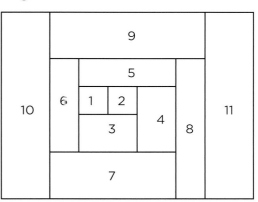

Fabric Covered Box

1 Following manufacturer's instructions, apply the double-stick fusible web to the wrong sides of the linen and lining pieces A–D. Set aside.

CREATE THE LOG CABIN TOP

2 Assemble the log cabin top using the cotton prints (#1–11) as follows and according to the diagram above.

3 Take pieces #1 and #2 and pin them right sides together, matching up the edges. Stitch them together down one side, then press the seam allowances toward #1.

4 Lay #3 on top of the seamed logs (#1/#2), right sides together, and aligning and pinning one long edge. Stitch along the pinned edge, then press the seam allowances toward #3.

5 Lay #4 on top of the seamed logs, right sides together lining up the edges as indicated in the diagram. Pin together and then stitch along the pinned edge. Press the seam allowances toward #4.

6 Continue adding the rest of the pieces in this manner until you have completed the log cabin top, using the diagram as a guide, and pressing the seam allowances toward the new piece added.

7 With the assembled log cabin top wrong side up, center the batting on top. There should be about 1½" (3.8 cm) of fabric left free on all sides of the batting.

8 Place the 7¼" x 5¼" (18.5 x 13.5 cm) book board on top of the batting. Brush PVA glue around the perimeter of the book board.

9 Roll the sides of the log cabin top over the edges of the batting and book board and press them onto the glue, following the instructions in the sidebar at left to miter the corners as you go. You have now encased the batting between the log cabin top and the book board. Set aside to dry.

CREATE THE BOX

10 Place the 9" x 11" (23 x 28 cm) book board on a table in front of you and with an acrylic ruler and a pencil, draw a rectangle that is 2" (5 cm) in from each edge. Then draw a 2" x 2" (5 x 5 cm) square at each corner of the book board. Cut out the corner squares with an X-Acto knife (**figure 1**).

11 Following the lines of the drawn rectangle, score the book board with the X-Acto knife to make creases. Be careful not to cut through the book board, you just need to be able to bend the sides.

12 Bend the sides of the book board up to form a box. Use masking tape (pieces about 2" [5 cm] long) to tape the corners together on both the inside and outside of each corner to hold the sides of the box together (**figure 2**). Use the bone folder to press the tape into the corners and make a nice flat crease.

13 Cut two 5" (12.5 cm) pieces of masking tape and use them to tape along the short edges along the outer bottom of the box. Cut two 7" (18 cm) pieces of masking tape and use them to tape along the long edges at the bottom of the box (**figure 3**). Make sure it's nice and flat!

COVER THE BOX

14 Peel the paper backing off of the linen strip. With the box laying on one side, stick the linen strip, centered, to the side of the box that is facing up, with about 1/2" (1.3 cm) of the linen hanging past the corner of the box. You should have about 3/4" (2 cm) of extra linen on each side of the

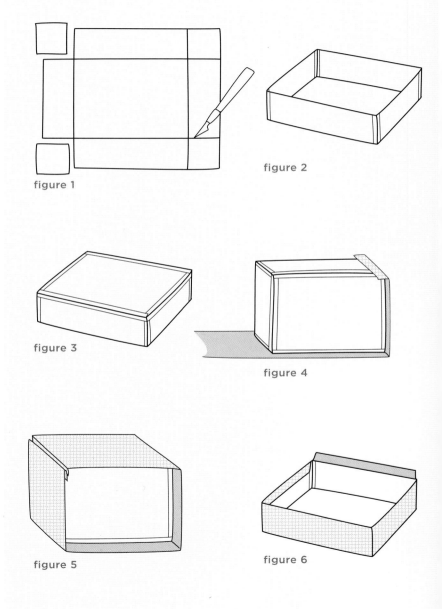

figure 1

figure 2

figure 3

figure 4

figure 5

figure 6

box (these will be folded over the top and the bottom edges of the box). Fuse the linen to the box with a hot iron (see manufacturer's instructions), smoothing as you go (see **figure 4**). Let cool before handling the box again.

15 Continue wrapping and fusing the linen onto the next 2 sides of the box, stopping when you reach the final side of the box. Fold the short raw edge of the linen under $1/2$" (1.3 cm) and press. Lay the linen down on the final side of the box and fuse as before, leaving about $1/2$" (1.3 cm) at the edge unfused. With a small paintbrush, apply a thin layer of PVA glue to the underside of the last $1/2$" (1.3 cm) of the linen and then firmly press it to the box and let dry (the edges of the linen will overlap so that none of the book board shows through; **figure 5**). The side with this overlapped "seam" will become the back of the box.

16 Turn the box so that the bottom is facing up and follow the instructions in the sidebar on p. 128 to miter the corners; folding the linen over the edges and fusing to the bottom of the box as you complete the mitered corners. Use PVA glue to fix the overlapped layers of linen at the corners to each other, as in Step 11.

17 Turn the box back over so that it is right side up and turn the $1/2$" (1.3 cm) flaps of linen into the box (except for the linen at the back of the box [the side with the "seam"]; leave this unturned) and fuse with a hot iron as before (**figure 6**).

ATTACH THE LID

18 Apply PVA glue to the outside of the flap that remains standing up at the back of the box (the glue should be on the side facing away from the box).

19 Take the lid you made earlier and center it over the top of the box for placement. Once it's centered, slip your hand under the lid and gently press the glued flap to the bottom of the lid. You can gently flip the box over so the lid lies on the table and smooth the flap against the lid to eliminate wrinkles and make sure it's secure. Let the glue dry before completing the next step (**figure 7** on p. 133).

20 Use the paintbrush to lightly brush some PVA glue onto the back of lining piece E. Be sure to cover the entire strip.

21 Center lining piece E, glue side down, over the point where the lid and the box meet so that half of it lies inside the box and the other half lies on the inside of the lid (**figure 8** on p. 133); press to secure and smooth with your fingers. Bend the lid back a little and press with your fingers along the crease to create some ease for opening and closing. Set aside to let the glue dry.

CREATE THE LINING

22 Match each lining piece with its corresponding chipboard piece (A–D). You should already have fused the fusible web to the wrong side of the lining pieces. Pull the paper off of the back of one of the lining strips. Center the corresponding chipboard over the lining piece and stick the board to the fabric. There should be $1/2$"

(1.3 cm) seam allowances left free on all sides of the lining piece; do not fuse the pieces together, this will be done in Step 20. Repeat to stick the remaining lining pieces to their corresponding chipboard pieces.

23 Clip the corners (p. 157) of each lining piece as close to the chipboard as possible.

24 Fuse the matched lining and chipboard pieces as follows:

A: Fold all edges of the lining over the chipboard and fuse.

B: Fuse the lining piece to the chipboard without folding over the edges (leave them flat).

C: Fold over only the long edges of the lining and fuse.

D: Fold all edges of the lining over the chipboard and fuse.

You now have the completed lining panels.

FINISH THE BOX

Refer to **figure 9** for assistance with the following steps.

25 Use the paintbrush to apply a thin layer of PVA glue to the inside of the lid, keeping it ¼" (6 mm) away from the edges. (PVA glue dries clear so don't worry too much if you get it too close to the edges.)

26 Quickly center and press lining panel A, right side up, onto the inside of the lid, over the glue. You can brush a little more glue under the corners if necessary. Press down evenly and smooth in place.

27 Next, brush PVA glue onto the bottom of the inside of the box, brushing the glue all the way to edges. Place lining panel B, right side up, down into the box, over the glue, allowing the fabric flaps to fold up along the sides of the box. Make sure the lining lies nice and flat in the bottom of the box.

28 Use your bone folder to help push the lining piece down into the box. Make sure you push the fabric into the creases where the lining flaps fold up the sides.

29 Now brush PVA glue onto the interior front and back sides of the box, brushing the glue over the linen fabric flaps as well. Try to keep the glue ¼" (6 mm) away from the top edge.

30 Place 1 lining panel C, right side up, on top of each of the glued sides of the box; one in front, one in back. Allow the flaps to fold along the sides of the box as before. Use the bone folder to help push the panels into place, making creases in the corners.

31 Brush PVA glue onto the two remaining sides on the inside of the box. Apply the glue from corner to corner, over the flaps of the 2 C panels from before. Try to keep the glue ¼" (6 mm) away from the top edge.

32 Place 1 lining panel D, right side up, on top of each of the glued sides of the box, using your bone folder to help push them into place.

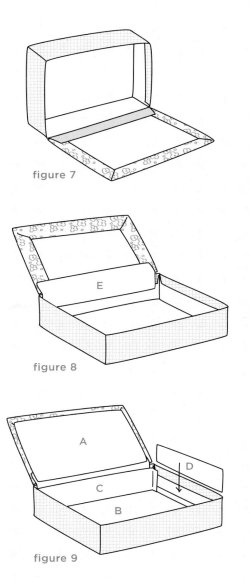

figure 7

figure 8

figure 9

33 Turn the box over so the bottom of the box is facing up. Brush PVA glue onto one side of the card stock, covering it completely. Center the card stock over the bottom of the box, glue side down. There should be ¼" (6 mm) of space around the card stock on all sides. Press and smooth the card stock and let it dry. All done!

16½" x 22½" (42 x 57 cm)

materials

For 1 towel

Linen *(shown: natural)*
  17½" x 23½" (44.5 x 58.5 cm)
  rectangle for towel

Various cotton prints *(5 different prints shown)*
  9 scraps, each at least 2¼" x
  2¼" (5.5 x 5.5 cm) for appliqué
  5¾" x 2" (14.5 x 5 cm) strip for
  the loop

Paper or card stock for
template

tools

Arc template (p. 150)

Blind hem or edgestitch foot
for sewing machine (optional)

kitchen TOWEL

Need to inject a little more fun into drying all those dishes? These delightful linen towels will do the trick! The inspiration for the patchwork motif at the edge comes from the traditional double wedding ring quilts I've always loved. Using a variety of bright cotton prints for the patchwork gives these towels a cheery presence that may just be the lift you need when you're in the midst of wash, rinse, dry, repeat.

Kitchen Towel

Note: All seam allowances are ¼" (6 mm) unless otherwise indicated.

1 Trace the Arc template onto paper or card stock (card stock will make a sturdier template) and cut out. Use a fabric marking pen or tailor's chalk to trace the Arc template onto the wrong side of each of the 9 cotton print scraps and cut out.

ASSEMBLE ARC APPLIQUÉ

2 Place 2 arc pieces, right sides together, lining up the edges. Sew together along one (straight) side, then repeat to attach another arc piece so that you have 3 pieces sewn together. Repeat entire step twice so that you have 3 arc segments.

3 Stitch the 3 arc segments together to make 1 large arc (see diagram at right for assistance).

4 Press all seam allowances to one side.

ATTACH ARC APPLIQUÉ TO LINEN

5 Fold the top and bottom edges of the completed arc appliqué (created in Steps 2–4) over by ¼" (6 mm), toward the wrong side, and press. Leave the short edges flat.

6 Lay the linen piece down flat in front of you, right side up, and place the arc appliqué on top at one corner (see the diagram, arc shown was placed at the bottom right corner). Place the arc appliqué so that each end is about 7¼" (18.5 cm) away from the corner, lining up the raw edges (adjust placement, if necessary, until the raw edges line up evenly); pin in place.

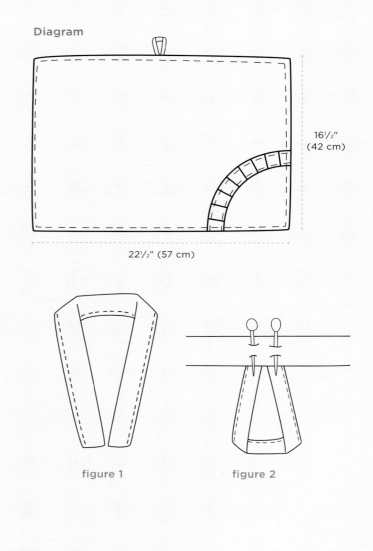

Diagram

16½" (42 cm)

22½" (57 cm)

figure 1

figure 2

7 Edgestitch (p. 154) the arc to the linen along the top and bottom edges and then press.

FOLD HEMS AND MITER CORNERS

8 Fold the hems on each side and miter the corners, according to the instructions under Creating Hems with Mitered Corners on p. 19, but fold the edges over by 1/4" (6 mm) instead of 1/2" (1.3 cm). Do not stitch the hems; this will be done in Step 12.

CREATE LOOP AND FINISH

9 Take the cotton piece for the loop and fold over each long edge 1/2" (1.3 cm), toward the wrong side, and press, then fold in half lengthwise so that the raw edges are encased inside and press. Edgestitch as close to the matched edges as possible, along the length of the strip.

10 Fold the strip in half, placing the ends next to each other to form a loop that will lie flat (**figure 1**).

11 On the wrong side of the linen piece, find the center of the top edge and slip the raw edges of the loop under the fold; pin in place (**figure 2**).

12 Edgestitch along the inside folded edge of the hems (about 3/8" [1 cm] from the outer edge; use a blind hem foot or an edgestitch foot if you have one). Press the towel and you're done!

finished size

About 9³/₄" (25 cm) tall
(not including straps) x 12"
(30.5 cm) wide at the base x 2"
(5 cm) deep (front to back)

materials

Linen *(shown: white)*
14¹/₂" x 24¹/₂" (37 x 62 cm) rectangle for shell

Various cotton print *(4 different
prints shown)*
14¹/₂" x 24¹/₂" (37 x 62 cm) rectangle for lining

9¹/₂" x 6³/₄" (24 x 17 cm)
rectangle for pocket

7¹/₂" x 7¹/₂" (19 x 19 cm) square
for large cloud

6" x 6" (15 x 15 cm) square for
medium cloud

5" x 5" (12.5 x 12.5 cm) for small
cloud

4 strips, each 2" x 17" (5 x
43 cm) for handles (use 2 different prints)

Fusible fleece
14" x 24" (35.5 x 61 cm)
rectangle

Light interfacing
7¹/₂" x 7¹/₂" (19 x 19 cm) square
for large cloud

6" x 6" (15 x 15 cm) square for
medium cloud

5" x 5" (12.5 x 12.5 cm) for small
cloud

Fusible interfacing
2 strips, each 1¹/₂" x 16¹/₂" (3.8 x
42 cm)

Paper or card stock for
templates

tools

Cloud templates (pp. 150 and
151)

Point turner (optional)

Blind hem or edgestitch foot
for sewing machine (optional)

cloud TOTE BAG

My little ones love to bounce around the house, carting a bag
filled with their favorite things. I created this bag with them in
mind. It's perfect for holding some coloring books and a few
favored toys, with a wide pocket in the back for crayons or
stickers. With cute cloud-shaped appliqués and soft straps that
are perfect for little shoulders, this tote is sure to be a hit with
the wee ones.

Cloud Tote Bag

Note: All seam allowances are ¼″ (6 mm) unless otherwise indicated.

1 Trace the Cloud templates onto paper or card stock (card stock makes sturdier templates) and cut out; set aside.

MAKE THE STRAPS

2 Lay out the 4 strap pieces (2″ x 17″ [5 x 43 cm]) and decide which print you want to use for the lining of the straps and place those 2 pieces wrong side up. Center the fusible interfacing pieces on top, fusible side down, and fuse according to manufacturer's instructions.

3 Fold over (toward the interfacing) each long edge of these straps by ¼″ (6 mm) and press. Repeat with the other set of straps (the second set will be the outer straps).

4 Place 1 lining strap and 1 outer strap wrong sides together (make sure the edges are still folded under so that no raw edges are showing) and pin. Edgestitch (p. 154) the straps together along each long edge. Repeat entire step with the remaining set of straps and then set both aside.

MAKE THE CLOUD APPLIQUÉS

5 Use a water-soluble fabric pen or tailor's chalk to trace the large cloud template onto the wrong side of the 7½″ x 7½″ (19 x 19 cm) cotton print square (do not cut out). Repeat with the medium cloud and the 6″ x 6″ (15 x 15 cm) cotton print square,

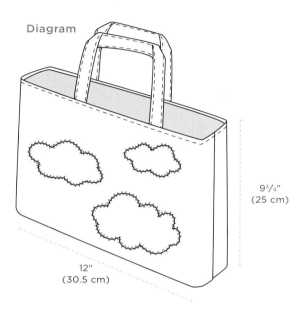

Diagram

9¾″ (25 cm)

12″ (30.5 cm)

and the small cloud and the 5″ x 5″ (12.5 x 12.5 cm) cotton print square.

6 Place the large cloud square right side down, on top of the corresponding interfacing square. Match up all edges and pin together through the center of the cloud. Repeat entire step with the medium and small cloud squares.

7 Stitching directly on your pen marks, stitch each cloud to the interfacing (**figure 1**). There are a lot of curves on the clouds so take your time and stitch slowly.

8 Trim the fabric and interfacing about ¼″ (6 mm) from the stitch lines on each cloud. Clip the seam allowances around the curves (p. 157), being careful not to cut

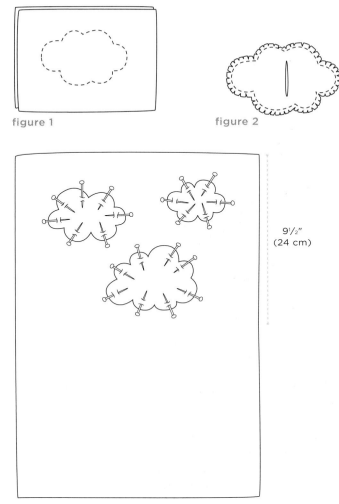

figure 1

figure 2

9½"
(24 cm)

figure 3

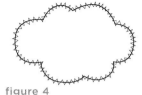

figure 4

through the stitching. This will make your curves a lot smoother when you turn the clouds right side out.

9 Remove the pins from each cloud. With an X-Acto knife or sharp scissors, gently and carefully cut a slit in the center of the interfacing only on each cloud (this will be used for turning; **figure 2**). Be careful not to cut into your cotton fabric.

10 Turn the clouds right side out through the slits, being careful not to rip the interfacing. Push the curves and dips out gently with the end of a blunt pencil or a similar-shaped object so that your cloud shape is crisp. This will take some maneuvering, so just take your time.

APPLY THE CLOUD APPLIQUÉS TO THE SHELL

11 Place the linen shell right side up in front of you, lying vertically so that the short edges are at the top and bottom. Arrange the clouds on the top half of the shell as desired (the bottom of the lowest cloud should be no more than about 9½" [24 cm] from the top edge so that they will be on the front of the bag; **figure 3**). Pin each cloud in place.

12 Set your machine to the zigzag stitch (consult your sewing machine manual for more information on settings for the zigzag stitch). If you've never used the zigzag stitch before, it is probably a good idea to practice on some scraps before continuing (you will be zigzagging around the edge of the clouds so practice using the stitch around curves). When using the zigzag stitch be sure to place the edge of the appliqué so that the right swing of the needle comes down just past the edge, into the base fabric. You want the needle to bounce back and forth from the appliqué to the base fabric so that the stitches cover the edges and also secure the appliqué to the base fabric (**figure 4**).

13 Slowly, zigzag stitch around each cloud, stopping to pivot the fabric at the end of each curve. Take your time to ensure that your stitches are neat and even around the edges of the clouds. You can either backtack (p. 154) at the beginning and end to secure or, alternatively, you can pull the thread tails through to the wrong side of the fabric and knot securely with double overhand knots (p. 156). Clip the thread tails.

14 Once all appliqués are attached to the shell, place the shell, wrong side up, in front of you. Center the fusible fleece on top, fusible side down and fuse it in place according to manufacturer's instructions.

CREATE THE POCKET

15 Take the cotton print pocket piece ($9\frac{1}{2}$″ x $6\frac{3}{4}$″ [24 x 17 cm]) and fold over one long edge (toward the wrong side) $\frac{1}{4}$″ (6 mm), then fold over another $\frac{3}{4}$″ (2 cm) and press. Topstitch (p. 155) along the folded edge about $\frac{5}{8}$″ (1.5 cm) from the edge.

16 Fold over the other long edge (toward the wrong side) $\frac{1}{4}$″ (6 mm), then fold over another $\frac{1}{4}$″ (6 mm); press. Repeat to fold each short edge.

17 Place the linen shell right side up in front of you, lying vertically so that the cloud appliqués are at the bottom and the opposite short edge is at the top. Center the pocket, right side up, on top of the shell, so that the hemmed edge of the pocket is $3\frac{1}{2}$″ (9 cm) from the top edge of the shell. Pin the pocket in place (see **figure 5**).

18 Topstitch the sides and bottom of the pocket to the shell, about $\frac{1}{8}$″ (3 mm) from

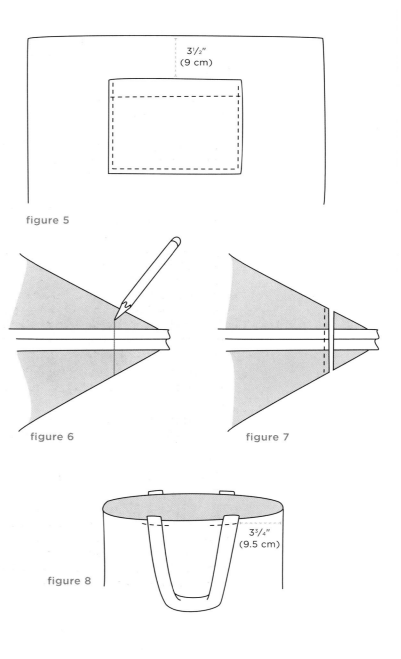

figure 5

figure 6

figure 7

figure 8

the edge, pivoting at the corners for a continuous stitch line. Leave the top open (**figure 5**).

ASSEMBLE THE BAG

19 Fold the linen shell in half widthwise, right sides together, lining up the top and side edges; pin together along the sides. Sew the side seams of the bag and then press the seam allowances open.

20 Flatten one side seam of the bag on the table so that it lies directly down the center, forming a point at the corner (**figure 6**). Using the acrylic ruler and fabric marking pen or tailor's chalk, measure about 1½" (3.8 cm) down from the corner and mark, then draw a line across the corner (perpendicular to the side seam), through the mark. Stitch along this line, then clip off the corner, about ¼" (6 mm) above the stitch line (**figure 7**). Repeat entire step for the opposite corner.

21 Turn the bag right side out. Push the corners out (use the point turner if necessary) and press.

22 Repeat Steps 20–21 with the cotton print lining (14½" x 24½" [37 x 62 cm]) and then set aside.

ATTACH THE STRAPS AND FINISH THE BAG

23 Place one raw edge of 1 strap onto the top edge of the shell bag, right sides together, placing the strap about 3¾" (9.5 cm) from the edge. Extend the raw edge of the strap about ¼–½" (6 mm– 1.3 cm) past the edge of the bag and then

pin in place. Repeat entire step to place the other edge of the strap. Repeat entire step again to place the second strap on the opposite side of the bag. Stitch across the end of each strap, ⅛" (3 mm) from the edge of the bag to secure them in place; remove the pins (**figure 8**).

24 With the lining still inside out, pull it up around the bag, aligning the side seams and top edges (right sides will be together). Pin together around the top edge.

25 You need to leave a gap for turning the bag right side out, so plan to leave this gap between the two ends of one of the straps. Stitch the layers together around the perimeter, starting just to the inside of one of the straps and stitching toward the side seam. Continue around the bag, ending just inside the opposite side of the strap from your starting point.

26 Turn the bag right side out through the gap and push out the corners (use the point turner if necessary). You may have to do a little tugging but be gentle so you don't rip any stitches.

27 Press the bag to get rid of any wrinkles from turning and to flatten the top edges of the bag. Turn in the seam allowances at the opening and press. Handstitch the opening closed with a slip stitch (p. 156).

28 Topstitch around the entire top edge of the bag, ¼" (6 mm) from the edge (be sure to keep both straps out of the way of the needle as you stitch).

materials

Linen *(shown: natural)*

8 squares, each 2³/₈" x 2³/₈" (6 x 6 cm) for table runner top

12¹/₂" x 20¹/₂" (31.5 x 52 cm) rectangle for table runner top

Various Cotton prints *(4 different prints shown)*

2 squares per print (3 prints) for zigzags, each 2" x 2" (5 x 5 cm)

7 rectangles per print (3 prints) for zigzags, each 2" x 3¹/₂" (5 x 9 cm)

12¹/₂" x 30³/₄" (31.5 x 78 cm) rectangle for backing (use fourth print)

2" x 101" (5 cm x 2.5 m) strip for binding (see Notes on p. 69 for further instruction)

Low-loft batting

13" x 31¹/₄" (33 x 79.5 cm) rectangle

tools

Hera marker

Walking foot for sewing machine (optional)

Bent-arm (quilting) safety pins (optional)

Table runners are a great way to dress up your dining table for special occasions or just for everyday use. I used a vintage bed sheet for the backing and binding of this runner, and I love the results. The zigzag patchwork pattern may look complicated, but you'll be surprised at how easy it is to make.

Zigzag Table Runner

Notes: All seam allowances are $1/4''$ (6 mm) unless otherwise indicated.

+ When piecing the triangles, squares, and rectangles for the zigzag panel, you will notice that the corners of the triangles will hang slightly past one edge of the square or rectangle it is being attached to. These will be covered with subsequent seams, but if you find them distracting as you sew, you can trim them flush with the edge of the square or rectangle after piecing the rows.

+ Using a large bed sheet for the binding on the table runner allowed me to cut a continuous strip for the binding. You'll probably need to cut several strips and seam them together end to end to obtain the 101'' (2.5 m) length of the binding. $5/8$ yd (57.5 cm) of 42–45'' (106.5–114.5 cm) wide fabric is sufficient to cut the binding strips, and the table runner backing ($1/4$ yd [23 cm] is sufficient if cutting binding strips only). Cut the strips 2'' (5 cm) long, across the width of the fabric (cut enough strips to obtain the necessary finished length), then follow the instructions under Patchwork Binding on p. 20 to complete the binding. Set aside the finished binding for use in Step 13.

CREATE THE ZIGZAG PANEL

1 To make the linen triangles that run along the zigzag section (see diagram A at right), cut each of the linen ($2^3/8''$ x $2^3/8''$ [6 x 6 cm]) squares in half diagonally from corner to corner with a rotary cutter and acrylic ruler (see Half-Square Triangles on p. 13 for assistance. You will have 16 triangles.

2 Lay out your cotton print squares (2'' x 2'' [5 x 5 cm]) and rectangles (2'' x $3^1/2''$ [5 x 9 cm]) and the linen triangles as shown in diagram B at right. Stitch each vertical row together; place 2 of the pieces right sides together, matching them up along one short edge, then pin and sew (when attaching the linen triangles, align the short edge of the rectangle or one edge of the square with one edge of the triangle so that the right edge of Rows 1–7 and the left edge of Rows 9–15 are straight; Row 8 will have both because there is a triangle at either end). Repeat as necessary to create each vertical row (see **figure 1** on p. 148 for an example of piecing the rows; shown: Row 2). Press all seam allowances up.

3 Once all of the vertical rows have been created, stitch the rows together in pairs, placing each pair right sides together and aligning one long edge (1 and 2, 3 and 4, 5 and 6, etc. . . .; see diagram B at right for assistance). Then, stitch the pairs to each other as before and be sure to add Row 15 onto the end of the zigzag panel. Press all seam allowances to one side.

ASSEMBLE THE TABLE RUNNER TOP

4 Take the linen table runner top piece ($12^1/2''$ x $30^3/4''$ [31.5 x 78 cm]) and lay it out in front of you, right side up. Using an acrylic ruler and a water-soluble fabric pen or tailor's chalk, measure and mark 4''

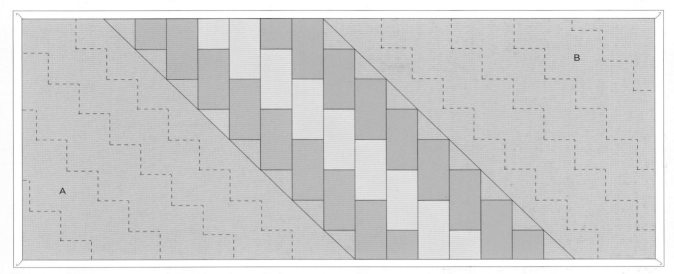

Diagram A

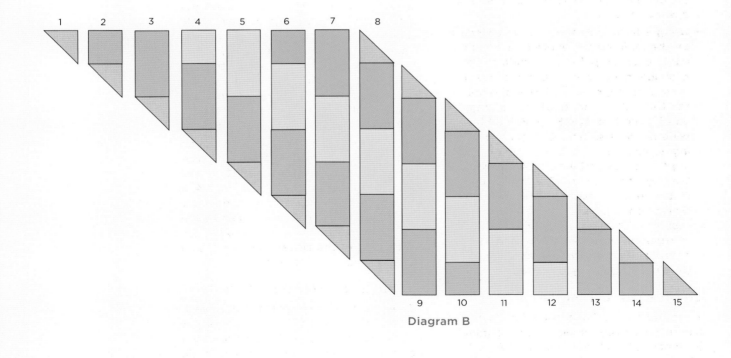

Diagram B

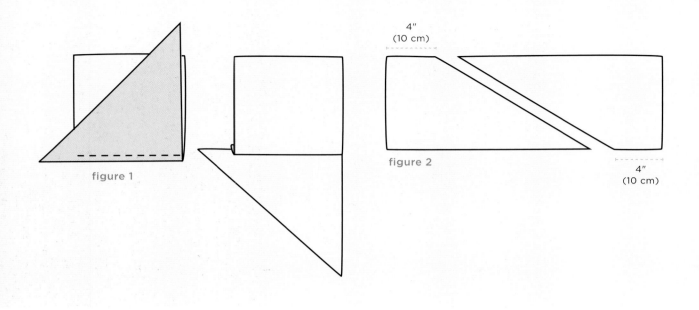

figure 1

figure 2

4"
(10 cm)

4"
(10 cm)

(10 cm) over from the top left corner and 4" (10 cm) over from the bottom right corner (see **figure 2**).

5 Draw a diagonal line from one mark to the other (be sure to use your ruler to draw the line). Use this line as your guide to cut the linen in half diagonally, using a rotary cutter (**figure 2**). Instructions below will refer to the left piece as A and the right piece as B.

6 Lay the zigzag panel in front of you, right side up. Place linen piece A (see diagram A) on top of the zigzag panel, right side down; line up the angled edges, and pin them together. Stitch together along the angled edge. Press the seam allowances toward the zigzag panel.

7 Repeat Step 6 on the other side of the zigzag panel with the linen B piece.

ASSEMBLE AND QUILT THE LAYERS

8 Use a hera marker and an acrylic ruler ruler to mark out the quilt lines on the assembled table runner top. Use the zigzag panel as a guide to make the first zigzag quilt line on the linen A piece, about 3" (7.5 cm) to the left of the zigzag panel or as desired (see diagram A). Repeat entire step to mark three more zigzag lines (or the desired number) on the linen, spacing each 3" (7.5 cm) apart and using the previous line as a guide. Repeat again to mark quilt lines on the linen B piece.

9 Layer the table runner pieces as follows: cotton print backing (right side down), batting (centered), assembled table runner top (right side up; be sure to place it directly in line with the cotton print backing). Hand-baste (p. 154) all of the layers together, basting in vertical rows no more than 6" (15 cm) apart. Alternatively, you can use bent-arm safety pins; place the safety pins in vertical rows as you would for hand-basting. There should be at least three safety pins to a row, with the rows no more than 6" (15 cm) apart (if you choose this option, just be careful when quilting and remove pins as necessary to keep them out of the way of the needle).

10 Beginning at the center (on the zigzag panel), use a walking foot and a straight stitch (p. 155) to machine-quilt the table runner by stitching in the ditch (p. 155) along the zigzag seam lines. Then, work your way out to the edge, quilting along the marked zigzag lines. Repeat to quilt the lines on the other side, working from the center, out to the edge. Remove the basting stitches with a seam ripper or remove the remaining safety pins.

BINDING AND FINISHING

11 Square up the edges of the table runner, according to the instructions under Squaring Up Quilts on p. 157.

12 If you have not yet created the binding, refer to the Notes on p. 146.

13 Bind the edges of the table runner and miter the corners as you go, according to the instructions under Attach Binding with Mitered Corners on p. 21. Use the walking foot to sew the binding if desired.

templates

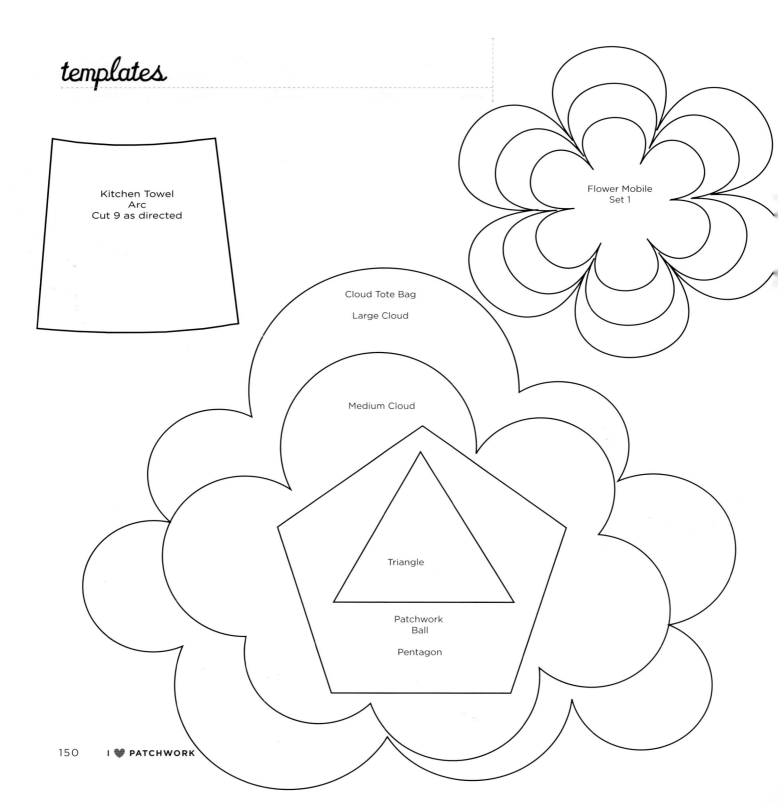

Kitchen Towel
Arc
Cut 9 as directed

Flower Mobile
Set 1

Cloud Tote Bag

Large Cloud

Medium Cloud

Triangle

Patchwork
Ball

Pentagon

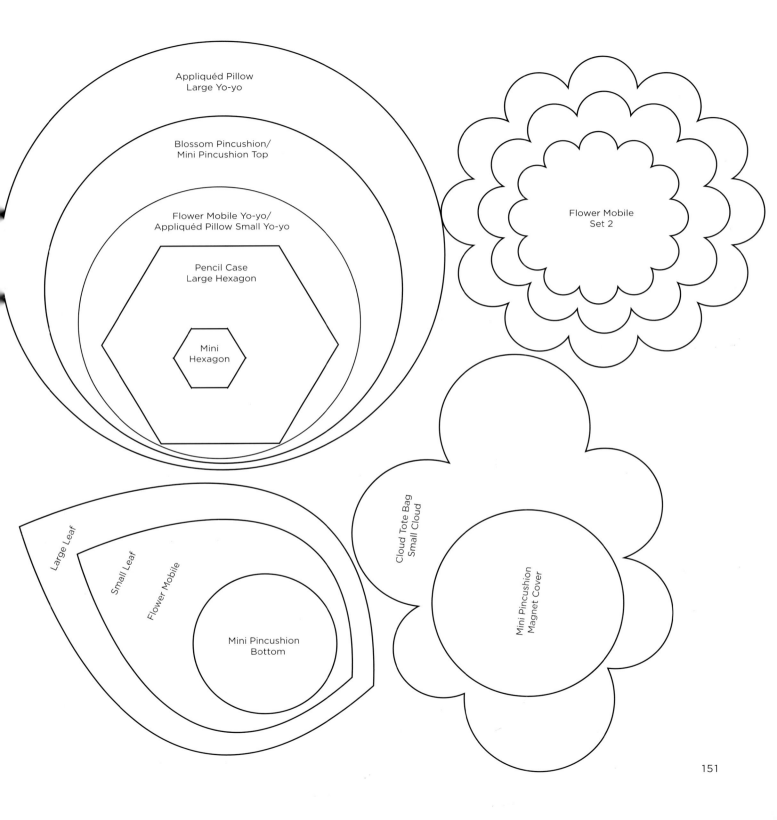

Appliquéd Pillow
Large Yo-yo

Blossom Pincushion/
Mini Pincushion Top

Flower Mobile Yo-yo/
Appliquéd Pillow Small Yo-yo

Pencil Case
Large Hexagon

Mini
Hexagon

Flower Mobile
Set 2

Large Leaf

Small Leaf

Flower Mobile

Mini Pincushion
Bottom

Cloud Tote Bag
Small Cloud

Mini Pincushion
Magnet Cover

little lamb softie pattern

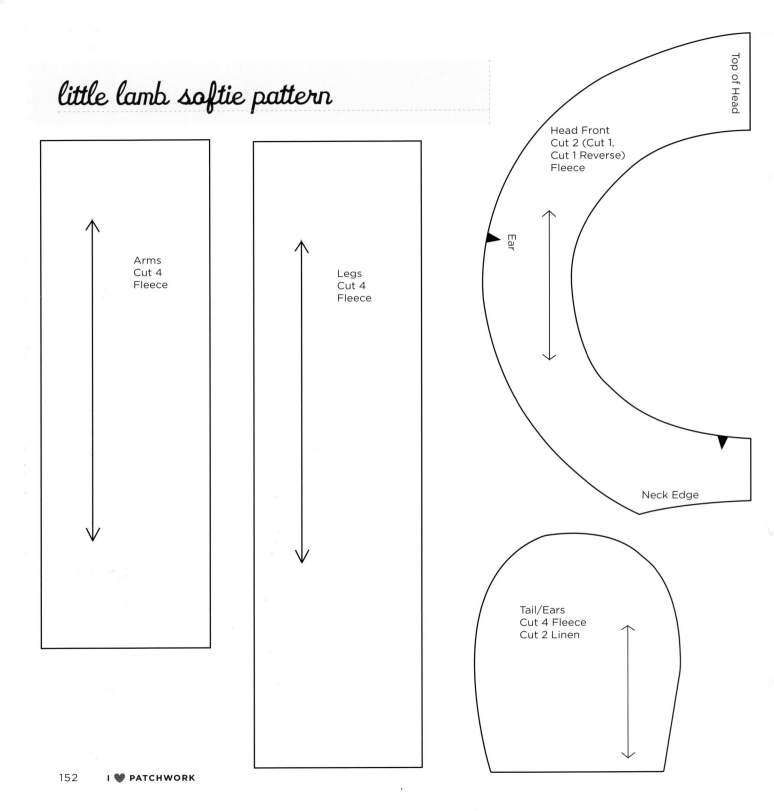

Arms
Cut 4
Fleece

Legs
Cut 4
Fleece

Top of Head

Head Front
Cut 2 (Cut 1,
Cut 1 Reverse)
Fleece

Ear

Neck Edge

Tail/Ears
Cut 4 Fleece
Cut 2 Linen

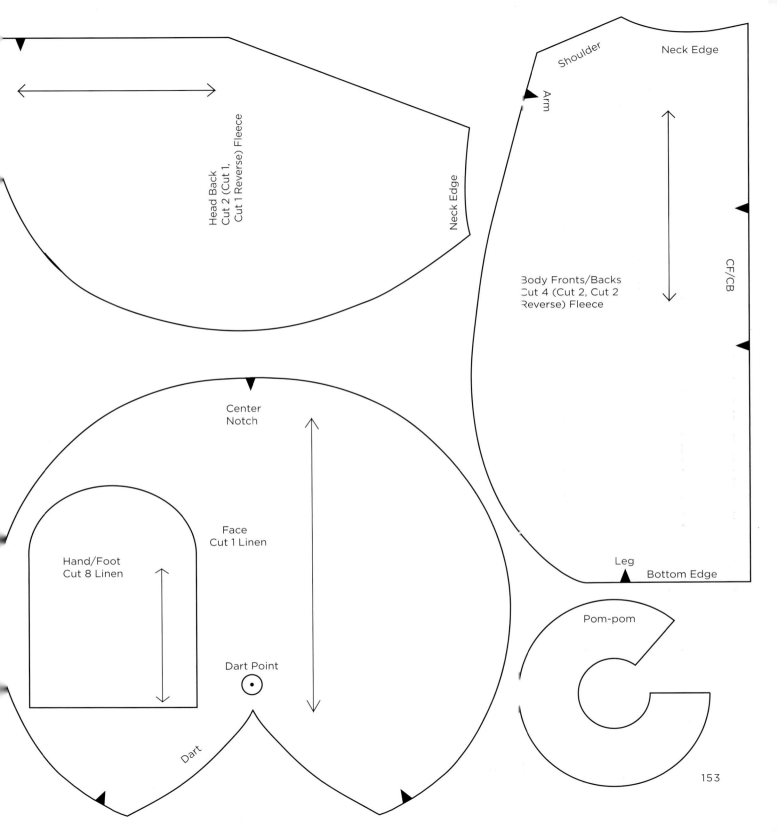

Head Back
Cut 2 (Cut 1,
Cut 1 Reverse) Fleece

Neck Edge

Shoulder

Neck Edge

Arm

Body Fronts/Backs
Cut 4 (Cut 2, Cut 2
Reverse) Fleece

CF/CB

Center
Notch

Face
Cut 1 Linen

Hand/Foot
Cut 8 Linen

Dart Point

Dart

Leg

Bottom Edge

Pom-pom

153

glossary

TERMS

Backtack: Sewing backward over previous machine stitching to secure it in place. This is usually done at the beginning and end of a stitch line. Most sewing machines have a backtack function; refer to your sewing machine manual for assistance with the settings on your machine.

Baste: Long, loose running/straight stitches used to temporarily secure a seam or other feature (such as gathers) in place and can be done by hand or by machine. The longer length makes them easier to remove when they are no longer needed. To **machine-baste**, set your machine to a long stitch length; to **hand-baste** use long running stitches, spaced about 1–2" (2.5–5 cm) apart for quilting and 1/4–1/2" (6 mm–1.3 cm) apart for other sewing applications.

Batting: Cotton, wool, or synthetic material that is placed as a filler between the layers of quilts and other projects. It is available in several thicknesses from low loft to super loft; projects featured in this book use low-loft batting.

Binding: A long strip of fabric used for covering the raw edges of quilts and other projects.

Edgestitch: A line of machine stitching that is placed very close to an edge or existing seamline, usually no more than 1/16–1/8" (2–3 mm) away. Using a blind hem foot or an edgestitch foot makes this much easier, as each of these feet have a guide that can be placed against the edge or fold to keep the stitching straight and even as you sew.

Fabric grain: The threads in a woven fabric that crisscross each other at right angles along the length and width of the fabric. The **lengthwise grain** refers to the threads that run along the length, parallel to the selvedges; the **crosswise grain** refers to the threads that run along the width, perpendicular to the selvedges. Straight grain refers to cutting fabric along the lengthwise or crosswise grain.

Fiberfill: Synthetic or natural fiber stuffing used for items such as dolls and pillows.

Finger press: Pressing a crease or fold by pushing firmly with your fingers instead of using an iron.

French seam: A seam in which the raw edges are enclosed on both the right and wrong sides of the garment or project.

Grainline: A line marked on a pattern that is used to line up the pattern with the straight grain of a fabric (grainlines are used to line up a pattern on the lengthwise grain, unless specifically marked as crosswise).

Interfacing: Fabric that is placed between the layers of a project to give it form and strength, available in fusible or sew-in versions in several weights.

Lining: Material used to hide the wrong side of a garment or project. Usually the lining is a mirror image of the shell.

Loft: The thickness of batting.

Machine quilting: Machine stitching that is made through two or more layers of a quilt or project for decorative as well as functional purposes.

Miter: A diagonal join or fold at a 90-degree corner in which the two edges meet at a 45-degree angle. Mitering corners on a sewing project gives you nicely finished points at the corners without extra bulk.

Notch: A pattern marking placed on the edge to indicate placement of an adjoining piece or other feature. Notches appear as small triangles against the edge of the pattern, with the point of the triangle facing in toward the pattern (see the Pattern Guide on p. 44).

Overlock stitch: A stitch used to finish the raw edges of fabric to prevent raveling, it can be produced with a serger, and a similar stitch, called an overcast stitch, can be produced with some conventional sewing machines. The zigzag stitch on a conventional sewing machine can be used as an alternative to finish the edges.

Raw edge: The cut edge of the fabric that has not yet been finished by seaming or hemming.

Right side: The right side of the fabric is the front side or the side that should be on the outside of a finished garment or project. On a print fabric, the print will be more visible on the right side of the fabric.

Running stitch: This basic handstitch is made up of evenly spaced stitches and can vary in length according to the instruction or as desired. Running stitches are used for decorative purposes and/or for joining pieces by hand in some cases. See also Straight stitch.

Seam allowance: The fabric between the raw edge and the seam.

Selvedge: The tightly woven borders on the lengthwise edges of the fabric that are created by the weaving process.

Shell: The material on the outside of a garment or project.

Stitch in the ditch: Stitching directly over a previous stitch line.

Straight stitch: This basic stitch is the default stitch on your sewing machine and is used for most common sewing applications. See also Running Stitch.

Topstitch: Stitching that is visible on the outside of a garment or project that is used to provide extra stability and/or for decorative purposes.

Wrong side: The underside of the fabric or the side that will be on the inside of a finished garment or project. On a print fabric, the print will be less visible on the wrong side of the fabric.

Zigzag stitch: A standard stitch function on most sewing machines that creates a zigzagging stitch line. This stitch is very versatile, with uses including decorative topstitching, reinforcement stitching, helping to prevent fraying at raw edges, and sewing on elastic or knit/stretch fabrics to allow for stretch. Refer to your sewing machine manual for more information on using the zigzag stitch function on your machine.

glossary

OVERHAND KNOT

Make a loop with the stringing material. Pass the cord that lies behind the loop over the front cord, then through the loop and pull snug.

BLINDSTITCH

Used for hemming or attaching an element when a virtually invisible seam is desired. Take a small stitch in one fabric at 1 (picking up only a few threads), then take the next stitch about $\frac{1}{8}$–$\frac{1}{4}''$ (3–6 mm) along in the other fabric at 2, creating a diagonal stitch; repeat until the seam is finished.

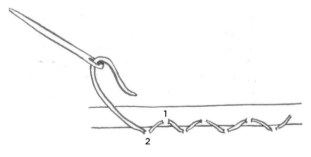

FRENCH KNOT

Bring the needle up at 1 and hold the thread taut about 2″ (5 cm) above the fabric. Point the needle toward your fingers and wrap the thread tautly around the needle twice (**figure 1**). Insert the needle into the fabric near 1 and complete the knot by holding the thread taut near the wrapped thread as you pull the needle toward the wraps and through the fabric (**figure 2**). **Figure 3** shows the completed knot.

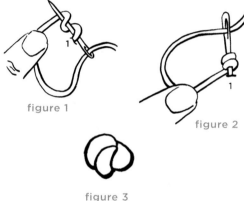

figure 1

figure 2

figure 3

SLIP STITCH

Take a stitch, about $\frac{1}{2}''$ (6 mm) long, into the folded edge of one piece of fabric and then bring the needle out. Insert the needle into the folded edge (or the fabric surface) of the opposite piece of fabric, directly across from the exit point of the thread in the previous stitch. Repeat by inserting the needle into the first piece of fabric, as before. This will create small, almost invisible stitches.

WHIPSTITCH

Bring the needle up at 1 and insert at 2, then bring up at 3. The stitches can be as close together or as far apart as you wish. Be careful not to make them too tight.

CLIP THE CORNERS

Clipping the corners of a project reduces bulk and allows for crisper corners in the finished product. To clip a corner, cut off a triangle-shaped piece of fabric, across the seam allowances at the corner. Cut close to the seamline, but be careful not to cut through the stitches.

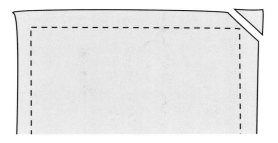

RUNNING STITCH

Working from right to left, bring the needle up and insert at 1, 1/8–1/4" (3–6 mm) from the starting point, then bring the needle up at 2. Repeat by inserting the needle 1/8–1/4" (3–6 mm) from 2 and continue as established.

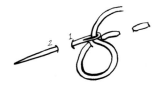

CLIP THE CURVES

Clipping the seam allowances along curved edges (concave or convex) reduces bulk and allows the seam to lie flat, eliminating puckering at the seamline. To clip the curves, make small, V-shaped cuts into the seam allowances along the curve (for concave curves, you can simply cut slits). Cut close to the seamline, but be careful not to cut through the stitches. Tighter curves will require more clipping, with the cuts spaced closer together than gentler curves.

SQUARING UP QUILTS

When you are creating a quilted project with a layer of batting in between the top and bottom layers, you will need to ensure that all layers are flush around the edges before you finish the edges (usually by binding them).

Place your quilt onto a self-healing mat and square up the edges by using a metal yardstick or a rigid clear gridded quilt ruler and rotary cutter to trim each edge as necessary so that all layers are even and the corners form neat right angles. Use the edge of the yardstick or ruler as a guide to make straight cuts with the rotary cutter.

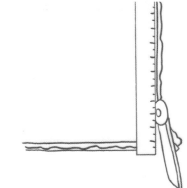

resources

Be sure to check your local fabric and quilt shops for fabric and supplies; many shops are also great sources of inspiration, displaying pieces by local artists or even traveling collections. Below are some of my favorite online resources.

COTTON PRINTS AND OTHER FABRIC

FAT QUARTER SHOP
PO Box 1544
Manchaca, TX 78652
(866) 826-2069
fatquartershop.com

J CAROLINE CREATIVE!
10801 Hammerly Blvd., Ste. 130
Houston, TX 77043
(866) 522-7654
jcarolinecreative.com

PURLSOHO.COM
(800) 597-7875
purlsoho.com

REPRODEPOT FABRICS
116 Pleasant St.
Easthampton, MA 01027
reprodepot.com

SEW, MAMA, SEW!
PO Box 1127
Beaverton, OR 97075
(503) 380-3584
sewmamasew.com

LINEN

FABRICS-STORE.COM
6325 Santa Monica Blvd., Ste. 102
Hollywood, CA 80038
(888) 546-3654
fabrics-store.com

GRAYLINE FABRICS
260 W. 39th St.
New York, NY 10018
(212) 391-4130
graylinelinen.com

LINEN ME
23 Glendale Close
St Johns
Woking
GU21 3HN
United Kingdom
linenme.com

TRIMS

WM. BOOTH DRAPER
2115 Ramada Dr.
Racine, WI 53406
(815) 648-9048
wmboothdraper.com

WOODED HAMLET DESIGNS
Needle & Thread
2215 Fairfield Rd.
Gettysburg, PA 17325
(717) 334-4011
woodedhamlet.com

JAPANESE FABRICS AND TRIMS

GOOD-NESS
alittlegoodness.etsy.com

MATATABI
matatabi.etsy.com

NUNO.+
nuno-plus.com

SUPER BUZZY
1932 Eastman Ave. #106
Ventura, CA 93003
(805) 644-4143
superbuzzy.com

SEWING SUPPLIES

CREATE FOR LESS
6932 S.W. Macadam Ave., Ste. A
Portland, OR 97219
(866) 333-4463
createforless.com

JO-ANN FABRIC AND CRAFT STORES
joanne.com

PAPER AND OTHER CRAFTY NEEDS

HOLLANDER'S
410 N. Fourth Ave.
Ann Arbor, MI 48104
(734) 741-7531
hollanders.com

PAPER PIECES
PO Box 68
Sycamore, IL 60178
(800) 337-1537
paperpieces.com

PAPER SOURCE
(312) 906-9678
paper-source.com

TSUKINEKO LLC
17640 N.E. 65th St.
Redmond, WA 98052
(425) 883-7733
tsukineko.com

INSPIRATION

Here is a list of some of my favorite blogs to visit when I'm in need of inspiration. There is some serious talent in this bunch!

ERLEPERLE.TYPEPAD.COM

JCHANDMADE.TYPEPAD.COM

OHFRANSSON.COM

PROVIDENCEHANDMADE.BLOGSPOT.COM

PURLBEE.COM

QUAINTHANDMADE.BLOGSPOT.COM

SMALLVILLESTUDIO.BLOGSPOT.COM

Visit my website at
IHEARTLINEN.TYPEPAD.COM

index

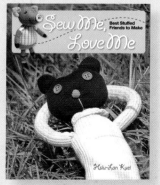